WHALE HUNTING WITH
GLOBAL ACCOUNTS

WHALE HUNTING WITH GLOBAL ACCOUNTS

Four Critical Sales Strategies to Win Global Customers

Foreword by Jill Konrath

BARBARA WEAVER SMITH

Printed in the United States of America

ISBN 978-0-9822091-7-2

The Whale Hunters, Inc.
3054 East Bartlett Place
Chandler, AZ 85249

www.thewhalehunters.com

Cover Design by Dejan Jovanovic
dejan.koki@gmail.com

Dedicated to whale hunters who go global

CONTENTS

FOREWORD

"Selling to big companies is tough. Really tough." That's how I kicked off my award-winning book, *Selling to Big Companies*, which came out in 2006. Ten year later, it's even more challenging.

And, it's hard to do well. Even getting started is filled with insurmountable obstacles – like finding out who might be involved in a decision, discovering how to connect with them and actually getting on their calendar. Today's executives protect their time zealously. Meeting with another self-serving salesperson (which is their typical perspective) is low on their priority list. Instead, they'd rather go online to learn about the issues they face, ways to address them and how similar buyers rate the various suppliers.

Since I wrote my first book, big companies are increasingly becoming multinational and global, and companies of all sizes from all parts of the world are competing for their business. Decision teams typically involve dozens of people with competing agendas, cultural differences and more.

The sellers who operate in this world need guidance. There are way too many ways to go wrong! That's why I was so pleased when Barbara asked me to be a contributor to her new book, and why, after reading it, I am delighted to introduce it to you.

This book is entirely new—it takes *Whale Hunting* to a whole new level of application, making it appropriate not only for small and midsize companies but also for global company sales teams and sales VPs who sell to other global companies. This is a deep dive into what it takes to be successful in the world of global sales, from how you structure your sales organization to how you can acquire the knowledge and skill to lead your global customer through a long and painfully complex decision cycle.

This book is decidedly strategic. It focuses on four key sales strategies to give you a competitive advantage:

- Gaining all the knowledge that you need,
- Finding an appropriate organizational structure for your global sales team,
- Following a disciplined, deliberate sales process that goes way beyond steps, and
- Keeping a vision in front of your client for the months or longer that a global sale will take.

I am intrigued by the method of this book, which marries advice from expert practitioners to Barbara's keen insights and her extensive experience guiding her clients to land whales. It works well and makes this book different from anything else that's out there. Very interesting perspectives!

Whether you are a global seller, a key account manager, a sales VP or a business owner bent on growth, you'll discover the right mix here of first-rate practice, good sense, and practical advice to take on the world of global sales. Whatever your role, buy this book and use it with your team.

Jill Konrath

Keynote Speaker | Sales Acceleration Strategist
Author: *Selling to Big Companies*, *SNAP Selling* and *Agile Selling*

PREFACE

Whale Hunting with Global Accounts is intended for C-level executives, Sales and Marketing leaders at all levels and Sales professionals who work with what I am calling "global accounts" in Business-to-Business companies. Your company may refer to them as "named accounts," "key accounts," "strategic accounts" or some other terminology. What's important here is that these accounts are special because they are large; they are complex; and more often than not, they are multinational or truly global. The book is written for leaders in companies of all sizes—global and multinational companies selling to others like themselves; small and midsize companies (SMBs) breaking in to global accounts or thinking about it.

Maybe you don't have a special approach to them yet—they are just your biggest customers. Or maybe you are thinking about whether you should approach a global prospect. Or even more likely you are working with one location of a huge company but not yet with other locations at home or abroad. It's time for you to think globally, before you lose business to a more enterprising competitor.

The Whale Hunting Process™ was laid out in my first book *Whale Hunting: How to Land Big Sales and Transform Your Company* (co-authored with Tom Searcy). Pick up a copy of that book, available in print, audio, or digital formats from amazon.com, if you have not read it previously. *Whale Hunting* describes a complete sales and business development process for SMB companies as they pursue bigger deals with bigger customers.

Whale Hunting with Global Accounts builds on that premise while taking *Whale Hunting* to a higher and more expansive level. In this book, you will find all new material as I drill down into the global whale hunt.

This expression of whale hunting is about the biggest whales of all, the global whales, and the sales and marketing teams around the world who do business with them. It focuses exclusively on the hunt. Although Whale Hunting is a suitable methodology for B2B companies in any industry, this book emphasizes the sale of services, not products, with examples drawn primarily from Information Technology, Business Process Outsourcing, Logistics, Training, and Pharmaceutical Consulting Services.

The Whale Hunting Process™ is derived from the analogy of how the Inuit people hunted whales centuries ago, on the northwest coast of what is now Alaska. After a whale was brought to shore and harvested, the Inuit returned its head, intact, to the Bering Sea.

The Inuit believed that the whales were reborn every spring. In this story, the whales are your global customers, and as a consequence of doing business with you, they will be reborn.

That is the degree of passionate attention the Inuit lavish on their whales. Their knowledge, structure, process and vision make them successful in breathing new life into their whales. I intend no less for you.

ACKNOWLEDGEMENTS

Thanks to the amazing members and sales industry stars of The Board, my mastermind group, who encouraged me on this venture and who provide priceless counsel to me in growing The Whale Hunters: Lisa Dennis, Dianna Geairn, Alice Heiman, Jennifer Leake, Lisa Magnuson, Carol Moser, and Laura Posey. They keep me on the path and make it all incredibly fun.

A big shout out to all the fine women members and leaders of Women Sales Pros—I am honored to call you my colleagues. Special thanks to Jill Konrath, founder, who chose me to be one of you and has become a remarkable friend and mentor.

Many thanks to Steve Harrison's awesome Quantum Leap program and National Publicity Summit, especially to Martha Bullen and Debby Englander for their editorial counsel and all of the deeply knowledgeable PR and marketing coaches.

My deep gratitude and love to Lawrence L. Smith, my partner in business and in life, who makes all things easier and makes me better at everything we take on together.

EXPERT CONTRIBUTORS

I am honored to include in this book the voices of fourteen experts from many influential positions in the world of global sales. They add multiple fresh, current perspectives from around the world; their passion for sales leadership shines throughout, and I am more grateful than words can say for their generosity.

Bios and photos of these contributors appear in ABOUT THE EXPERT CONTRIBUTORS.

Rachel Barger, GM EMEA & Global Head Customer Success and Value Engineering Lithium Technologies, Zurich, Switzerland

Valerie Bonebrake, SVP, Tompkins International
Raleigh, NC and Kansas City, KS USA

Tiffani Bova, VP, Distinguished Analyst and Research Fellow, Gartner, Los Angeles, CA USA

Melissa Donnelly, VP of Sales, JDA
Dallas, TX USA

Gerhard Gschwandtner, Founder and CEO, *Selling Power* Magazine and Sales 2.0 Conferences
Fredericksburg, VA USA

Jeff Hargroves, President, ProPharma Group, LLC
Kansas City, Kansas USA

Matt Heinz, President, Heinz Marketing
Seattle, WA USA

Jill Konrath, Keynote Speaker, Award-Winning Author, Sales Accelerator, Minneapolis, MN USA

Sid Kumar, Global Head of Inside Sales, CA Technologies New York, NY USA

Lisa Magnuson, Founder and Corporate Sales Strategist, Top Line Sales, Portland, OR USA

Kirk Robinson, SVP Commercial Markets Division & Global Accounts, Ingram Micro, Orange County, CA USA

Mircea Saracut, Head of Business Development—EMEAA, Symbicore, Cluj County, Romania

Hari Shankaranarayanan, Managing Director with a leading management consulting services company, New Dehli, India

Dr. Greg Story, President, Dale Carnegie Training Japan Tokyo, Japan

Please note: Quotations have been modified for length, clarity, and consistency with precursor material. All quotations maintain the intent of the expert contributors, who were provided with the opportunity to review and revise their words in the manuscript. All opinions are those of the individuals themselves and do not represent the views of the companies for whom they work.

Places of employment were correct as of document preparation, but of course are subject to change.

INTRODUCTION

This book is about becoming the kind of sales organization that is not willing to do tomorrow what you did yesterday. It's about sales leaders who cut through the bureaucracy and get things done. Sales teams and marketing teams who are fiercely determined to become more successful in opening new large accounts and driving new business with their current global accounts.

I set out to supplement my own knowledge and experience with large account sales by interviewing fourteen sales experts, whose voices are prominent throughout the book. In this way I intended to create a book that would feature current, relevant advice and challenges, through the personal experiences of today's global account sales practitioners as well as my own.

My clients are frustrated with their progress on large account and global account sales. Both the company management team and the sales representatives who work with global companies believe that they don't know the most productive ways to use their time and that they don't close opportunities as often as they want to, in the way they intended to. The larger the accounts and the more complex the sale, the more dissatisfaction companies express about sales to their global accounts.

There is ample research evidence to support my own experiences with my clients.

A summary of several findings from "The State of Sales Execution," *Sales Execution Trends 2015* (Qvidian) included:

- Top reasons for not reaching quota: "no decision" and "sales can't communicate value"
- 50 % of salespeople fail to meet quota, year over year (from *Top Sales World)*
- Inability to identify and gain access to decision makers
- Lack of understanding of the buying process

> *"The disconnect between what the buyer wants and what the sales rep provides us is at the crux of a persistent problem: the strategy and sales execution gap."*

Astonishingly, one study reported that B2B sellers have the opportunity to meet with a qualified buyer only *twice a year* and that they strike out 70% of the time in those meetings. Consequently, the immediate opportunity is lost 59% of the time. A key reason for this failure is lack of sales and marketing alignment, although as you can imagine, there is no consensus between sales and marketing about what is the problem. (*The Metrics of Bad Sales Interactions: A Sales Experience Benchmark Report.* Demand Metrics, July 2014.)

Mark Lindwall (Forrester) reports that "your only true differentiator comes from how your reps interact with your buyers." The advantage goes to those who deeply understand the buyers' roles and business challenges and bring them genuine ideas on how to solve the challenge. Forrester asked a question of B2B buyers, "How often do you choose a vendor who has worked with you to turn a vision into a clear path to value?" The response was "74% of the time" (*Q4 2012 Global Executive Buyer Insight Online Survey*).

Companies of all sizes repeatedly go after large accounts, which are often multinational or global accounts, and end in failure or settling for a much smaller opportunity, or a much less advantageous opportunity, than the one they originally hoped to close. Nevertheless, companies of all sizes can land and serve global accounts to the advantage of their customers and themselves with the proper preparation and execution.

I wrote this book to help you become much more successful in initial sales and repeated sales to global accounts, to actually get into their global locations, not just the plant or R&D Center or subsidiary closest to you. It is not a theoretical book, nor is it a step-by-step how-to book. Rather, it is a practical discussion of how you can close that gap between what the buyer wants and what you, the seller, provide.

Four Critical Business Sales Strategies

As this book came together, I distilled four critical strategies of selling to global accounts through my interviews and client experiences. You need to develop all four areas in comparable depth and attend to how customers' expectations have evolved. The book is therefore organized into these four strategic areas:

- **Knowledge**. Global account salespeople need a massive store of knowledge about their target company and its market, as well as about its industry and business challenges. And there's much more. It is amazing to hear story after story, and to see in my own experiences with clients, how sales reps go in to a meeting with an executive at a global company, armed only with product knowledge and product materials. Nothing is more fundamental than broad and deep knowledge about your customer's world.

- **Structure**. You will not be successful at selling to and serving large, complex organizations unless you are carefully organized on your own side. But the way you structure your sales operation must arise from a deep understanding of your customer's needs and preferences. I offer many structural examples and discuss how to determine which is most appropriate for your company at a particular stage in your growth.

- **Process**. Many successful sales teams follow well-crafted steps to undertake a sale and carry it through to closure. The more complex the sale, however, and the longer the sales cycle, the more likely it is that salespeople are following their own intuition about what the buyer is thinking. What constitutes a successful process is changing rapidly and dramatically, as the buyers' journey becomes far more fluid and less linear than steps can represent.

- **Vision**. Maybe it's a word too well-worn, but vision is the path to an exceptional value proposition for your customers. Simply put, vision is a detailed picture of how certain business circumstances will be much improved at some future time. Your vision needs enough power to lead your customers through the problems of consensus-building, the pain of change, and the inertia of bureaucracies.

Armed with these four strategies, you will gain a competitive advantage in the global sales arena.

PART I

KNOWLEDGE: LOOK DEEPER

WHALE HUNTING PERSPECTIVES

Whale hunters ancient and modern know more about their whales than most people know about anything. They are students of the whale and whale behaviors, and they are teachers and mentors to the youth who are their future whale hunters. They spend an extended time in preparation in comparison to the actual duration of the whale hunt.

The first steps in Whale Hunting are to locate whales that may be suitable for you and select the ones that you believe will be a good fit. Once you've made an initial selection, you research the candidates and once again reduce the pool of potential customers for you. This process will be repeated at intervals, whenever you are ready to find more whales—in a new market, for example—or whenever a new whale asks for your attention.

I begin with the assumption that you have already identified global whales, large global accounts that require special attention from your company. You already have a few such accounts, or perhaps you have many, and you have a global sales team or expect to put one in place.

I'm meeting you at a point in your sales process when you need to learn a lot more about a particular account because the account is new, you are new to the account, or simply that you must learn more in order to do your best work with this whale. This section is about how you can develop deep knowledge about global accounts and use your knowledge to help them make excellent business decisions.

Everyone says—"make your sales decisions to best serve your customers" – "it's all about your customers" – "deliver to your customers' preferences." I hear and read volumes of lip service to that concept. But what does it really mean? How do you really do it? If you are going to organize your global sales organization deliberately around your customers, you had better start with knowing a lot about your customers, who they are today, and what are their aspirations for the future.

What are the unique features of global accounts? What makes them so different from smaller or local accounts or even national accounts? What unique business issues do they have? And most important, what do they expect from you? Those are the issues I tackle in this section.

CHAPTER 1

YOU DON'T KNOW ENOUGH

I worked with a fast-growing software company whose sales reps were extremely skilled at building relationships with their customers. As the company grew, they did more business with much bigger companies, and still their best sales reps built rough-and-ready relationships— when they went to visit they took their clients out for drinks, dinner, golf outings, parties at the trade shows. They were buddies, right?

They landed one deal with a global whale. As they got to know the buyers' group, it was sales as usual. All about relationships, friendships, and party time. But what they didn't know is that the leaders of this much larger company did not want their buyers and end users hanging out with the sales reps. They thought it was all much too cozy, and at a critical point my client lost that big company's business not in spite of relationships but because of them. They focused on the ones who they perceived to be in charge and completely failed to read the signs of a new order.

That story exemplifies failure to know your customer. The sales reps thought they knew, but they only knew a particular set of people who were no longer well-regarded among leaders in their own company, in part because of the nature of the relationships they had developed with a sales team. Management was listening only to the sales reps' stories and promises; they had no process to solicit independent verification from management of the customer account.

Everyone will tell you that sales are built on relationships, but that's trivial. What kind of relationships? With whom? To what end? In this case, a good relationship with the wrong people through the wrong behaviors killed the opportunity for long-term business.

If you are dealing with a global customer, I'm betting you don't know enough!

If somebody knows enough, that knowledge hasn't made its way into all the right heads. And if everybody knows a piece of enough, you don't have a reliable way to gather that knowledge and disperse it among your extended teams of sales and marketing and operations and customer service and training and finance and development and whoever else touches the customer.

You must develop a deep understanding of a global company – its industry, its market, its competitors, and especially its strategy and business issues. It's extremely difficult to differentiate yourself and your company's services in the global customer market; superior attention to the customer's business is a primary way to do so.

I am convinced that most companies, through their sales teams and beyond, are woefully unprepared and under-prepared to make and manage sales to a global customer, in part because they simply don't take the time to know enough about the customer prior to important meetings and milestones.

The global companies I am talking about are whales—they are large AND they are global. If you approach them properly and serve them well for a long time, your opportunity for more business with that whale is unlimited. Repeat business with a global whale can be an anchor for your company. But whales are unforgiving to amateurs, which is how your team will appear if you just don't know enough.

Whale Hunting companies grow their businesses deliberately by selling bigger deals to bigger customers. You continue to do the kind of business that you do now, but your average customer size and your average deal size continue to grow. Soon some of your smaller accounts drop off—maybe you will hand off smaller accounts to a strategic partner or create a new division.

As you grow and encounter global accounts, a new challenge is to understand how a global company works and how much opportunity it really represents for you. In other words, could you do *whale-sized business* with a global whale? Knowledge is where to start.

Getting to Know a Global Whale

Marketing has become focused on personas, which are representations of the demographics and buying behaviors of your actual or ideal customers. Personas are people—not organizations. But when you are dealing with a global organization, you can use the persona concept to develop a complete picture of that corporation—what is it like as a business. This must happen before you start to talk with people who run the business.

The corporate persona for a global customer should include:

- **The Big Picture**. You need to know the corporation's size and structure, history, primary locations, and the industry or industries in which it operates. Learn also its markets, competitors, financial picture, and reputation. Find out what they do, how they do it, and where.

- **The Corporate Family**. A corporation doing business globally consists of multiple entities that are owned by or "held" by the corporation. You need to know all relevant members of the corporate family – especially major divisions, subsidiaries, and business units that have their own profit-and-loss responsibility.

- **The Corporate Strategy**. What are the executives and board trying to accomplish in the next one year, three years, five years? Know their major corporate initiatives, plans, goals, opportunities, and those of their major corporate family entities.

- **Industry and Competitors**. What's going on in the industry? Is it expanding or contracting? Where is the most activity, globally? What are the issues? Know their major competitors and how they stack up against the competition. How do they differentiate? Who wins most of the business?

- **Which Doors to Open**? You need to make a strategic decision about where and how you want to introduce yourself. This decision includes a location, a level of seniority, a functional area, a business unit—and other considerations as well. It's hard to move up or even to move out from the people with whom you first talk. Make sure that is a serious, well-planned decision. If you're already in there, start from where you are.

Make it unacceptable for your team to call on any company or company subsidiary without having a complete picture of who they are! Everyone in your company who would interact with this prospective global customer, anywhere or any time, should know that big picture.

The Big Picture

To be specific, let's explore Novartis AG, a publicly traded company on the New York Stock Exchange, headquartered in Basel, Switzerland. Novartis is an outstanding example of the complexity of a $60 billion global corporation and what your sales team would have to know about it in order to do repeat business with them globally. Here's a brief summary for starters:

"Novartis AG provides healthcare solutions. The Company is a multinational group of companies specializing in the research, development, manufacturing and marketing of a range of healthcare products led by pharmaceuticals. Its portfolio includes medicines, eye care, cost-saving generic pharmaceuticals, preventive vaccines and diagnostic tools and over-the-counter products. It has five operating segments: Pharmaceuticals, which include patent-protected prescription medicines; Alcon, which include surgical, ophthalmic pharmaceutical and vision care products; Sandoz, which include generic pharmaceuticals; vaccines and diagnostics, which include human vaccines and blood-testing diagnostics; and consumer health, which include over-the-counter medicines."

—AS REPORTED BY AVENTION "ISELL" SUBSCRIPTION SERVICE, APRIL 10, 2015. ORIGINALLY CREDITED TO REUTERS

Essentially, Novartis is five separate companies operating under one corporate banner. They do things as one corporation, and they do things as five companies. And many combinations in between.

As of this writing, Novartis had a corporate "family" of 375 companies. Three hundred seventy-five companies within one global corporation; it's a lot to understand. But if you are going to sell into any part of Novartis, your sales team needs a working knowledge of its corporate structure and the companies that make up its portfolio. Novartis was formed originally by a merger and has completed many acquisitions as well as divestitures. For example, in late 2014 Novartis sold its Novartis Animal Health division to Elanco, which is owned by Eli Lilly and Company. If you were doing business with Novartis Animal Health at the time, the future of that business was suddenly up in the air. You also would need to start learning a lot more about Eli Lilly and Elanco, its animal health division, which now owns a big piece of what was once Novartis.

In Whale Hunting language, Novartis is a whale, no matter who *you* are. Even if you represent a company as big and as complicated as Novartis, you still face a high degree of complexity in making a sale to them. The more strategic your service is to Novartis, the more complex a sale is likely to be.

Know the Corporate Family

Quite possibly, you will begin your relationship with Novartis at one of their subsidiary companies or a branch office. Suppose your company, like my expert contributor Jeff Hargroves' company, sells a wide variety of compliance and engineering consulting and outsourcing services to the pharma industry. Maybe you have a presence in Atlanta, Georgia, and you are hoping to do business with Alcon Laboratories, the largest subsidiary of Novartis, which employs 2500 people in Georgia with annual revenues of $607 million. That component of Novartis alone may be considerably larger than your company, and certainly they could do many whale-sized deals with you.

But before you call on Alcon in Atlanta, wouldn't you want to know that Alcon Labs has 4500 employees at its headquarters location in Texas, plus close to 1000 employees working in each of its operations in California, Texas, and Illinois, and similar clusters of employees in other locations in the United States, plus branches and subsidiaries all over Europe and in most parts of the world? Knowing that helps you to decide whether you have a service only for a single branch or, perhaps, for multiple locations of the company.

Many of The Whale Hunters' clients could and would be doing business with a company like Alcon Laboratories in Georgia. But they would be coming to The Whale Hunters to learn how to do business with all of Alcon Laboratories—or all of Alcon in the United States— or even all of Alcon's manufacturing facilities or warehouses or R&D operations. And they would start by learning all about Alcon, and its parent company Novartis, to make the right kinds of decisions about how to organize themselves in order to serve Novartis or any of its family of companies.

The Corporate Strategy

In order to have a serious business discussion with a Novartis or Alcon or Sandoz executive, it helps to have some background about their current corporate strategy. What does the company intend to accomplish in the next year or two-to-three years? Each company in the portfolio, each executive in each of the companies, each manager reporting to the executives has a specific responsibility for achieving the corporate strategy. You have to know something about that before you ever have a conversation with anyone.

I Googled "what is Novartis' corporate strategy" and found the summary of an investors' meeting that company executives held in June 2015. They discussed what they had accomplished with a strategic realignment of their portfolio, both divestitures and acquisitions. Next they intend to "strengthen innovation" across the three primary businesses—Novartis, Alcon and Sandoz.

You would have to find out what they mean by strengthening innovation and how that relates to the job expectations of people with whom you'd like to talk, as well as how potentially it could relate to your business services or products, in order to have a sensible conversation with a key person at Novartis or the subsidiaries

In the same meeting summary, key news for sellers was the announcement of Novartis Business Services (NBS), the company's new shared services organization that covers approximately $5 billion in spend. This new organization will influence how Novartis and its divisions buy all kinds of products and services. As a company that wants to make them a customer, you will have to learn and understand how this works. [Novartis Executives Outline Strategy and Cost-Savings Initiatives, Patricia van Arnum, June 2015].

Industry and Competitors

To understand an industry, refer to several sources to uncover attitudes and points of view. When the World Health Organization writes about pharmas, it notes that companies "spend one-third of all sales revenue on marketing their products - roughly twice what they spend on research and development." [WHO website retrieved 12/05/15.] WHO, a nonprofit organization, is concerned about what it believes to be a conflict of interest between pharma companies and the public. On the other hand, PWC emphasizes the "harsh commercial environment" and identifies three key issues facing companies: "Rising customer expectations, Poor scientific productivity, and Cultural sclerosis." [PWC website retrieved 12/05/15].

Depending upon which source you read, you will get a different picture of the industry. So read more than one and draw your own conclusions. Try to figure out how your target company is positioning in the industry environment. Are they trying to partner with WHO or other nonprofits to build their reputation for being concerned about the public? Or do they align with their peers in addressing the harsh industry circumstances?

As you learn the industry, you'll have to figure out how your company's products and services fit with major threats and opportunities, as well as anticipating the difficulty of working with an outmoded culture or the chance to help a company change its culture, if that's your business.

As a major pharmaceutical, Novartis has a significant number of peer organizations and literally hundreds of competitors. Several of them are probably better known to you than Novartis—Johnson & Johnson, Bayer, Pfizer, Merck. When I'm researching the competitors of a Global 500 company, I usually look for articles about the Top 25 or Top 10 in a particular industry. Sometimes I find a good discussion of the company amongst its competitors, including their relative ranking positions over a few years' time. I located several such articles about Novartis.

Which Doors to Open?

If you have your eye on Alcon, do you want to sell only in Georgia, or do you want multiple Alcon locations to do business with you? Explore these possibilities early in your relationship with the first Alcon location. Discover how they make purchasing decisions for your services or products. Does each subsidiary purchase for itself, or each branch, or is there a centrally managed system? Does Alcon manage its own procurement or does it outsource?

If you sell enterprise technology, learn what Alcon considers to be scope of their enterprise. It may be one location, or all of Europe, or all of the world. Perhaps they are grappling with a way to make their enterprise systems seamless across all of the subsidiaries to maximize customer knowledge, to improve research collaboration, to reduce costs, or to increase the value of what customers get for their money. The same possibilities may also exist not only for enterprise technology but also for such disparate products and services as branding and marketing, logistics and transportation, business process outsourcing, supplies, commercial real estate, construction, and countless others.

As you begin to research and analyze opportunities with Alcon, go up to the bigger picture. How is Alcon's corporate strategy intertwined with that of the parent company, Novartis? Understanding Novartis will help you get a handle on Alcon. Some corporate decisions at Alcon require ultimate approval by Novartis. What does that mean for your business with Alcon from a communication and culture perspective? A corporate headquarters in Switzerland behaves differently from a corporate headquarters in India or China or the United States. They are all different in multiple ways—more or less risk averse, more or less top down, more or less distributed decision-making.

How to Learn About Them

The Whale Hunting way to understand your customers' business, their strategy, their issues and more starts with disciplined study and eventually yields deep understanding of their business. "You" means "your company" and "you yourself," no matter your role.

Three functions are required to complete this work and keep it up to date:

1 **Scouting**: conducting research and maintaining up-to-date information

2 **Communication**: sharing and circulating information and pertinent updates

3 **Tools**: supporting the collection of and easy access to pertinent information

If you are a senior executive in sales, marketing, operations, IT, or customer service, you have a role in making sure that these functions are funded, that IT tools are provided, and that lines of communication flow through your area to and from the others. If you are only responsible for sales, and senior management does not see this as a role for them, you should negotiate with your peers to ensure that this work is accomplished routinely. And if you are a sales rep and you are not provided with the appropriate information or do not have opportunities to communicate with peers in other functional areas, I suggest you lobby for these services or do the work yourself for a few key global accounts.

Scouting

In whale hunting terminology, "scouts" are the ones who manage the research about whales. Doing the research is not the job of a salesperson; it's not typically their long suit nor is it a good use of their time. Studying the research is definitely a sales rep's job, but gathering and organizing is a sales support, or marketing, or sales enablement function, whatever you choose to call it. You need someone who has the time and who really likes the digging and making connections that the research process requires.

My earlier book, *Whale Hunting,* includes detailed information on how to manage the Scouting process, starting from the very beginning with defining your ideal whale by means of a *Target Filter.* For our purposes now, I'm assuming that you have decided on a potential target or that you have even sold into the target company once or more.

Start with the big picture and drill down from there, completing all of the details identified as part of a corporate persona. Your Scout can conduct do-it-yourself research starting with the corporate website and branching out through Internet searches.

For publicly-traded companies listed on the New York Stock Exchange, read their Security and Exchange Commission (SEC) filings, especially the 10-k annual report, focusing on the business summary and the management discussion and analysis (MD&A). You will learn more strategic detail than what is typically included in an annual report. These documents are public and are readily available on the company's website or through the SEC online; they are required for both domestic and foreign companies.

If you do not have the capacity to do this research on your own, outsource your research to an independent contractor or an industry-specific research company that for a fee will conduct account profiles, detailed research reports on a company or one of its lines of business or a single geographic area. If you want to create customized corporate personas from companies in multiple industries, visit thewhalehunters.com/research to learn how we can help.

In addition to gathering information from a powerful comprehensive research database, Scouts should be curious. Sales reps should also ask Scouts for specific information that would be helpful. Do a Google search on questions that matter specifically to your business, for example:

- *What is Novartis training budget?* I came across an article on their Corporate Learning brand, with many insights on how they provide continuing education for their top 10% executives plus all the other ways they provide training including through about 450 training provider companies and individuals, using about 150 outsiders each year.

- *What software does Novartis use*? I discovered a new joint venture with Qualcomm Life that uses wireless technology to collect patient data digitally during clinical trials. This is an enormous step ahead in healthcare/technology applications.

- *How does Novartis handle logistics?* I found an article from 2012 announcing that IJS Global opened a dedicated warehouse in the Philippines to handle logistics for Novartis Animal Healthcare.

Plug your own topics and services into this format. Search for simple questions about your industry, things you do, opportunities that would interest you, and you'll get an idea of what's going on at your dedicated global accounts and prospects.

Tools

I'm not going to provide a list of resources for conducting research about global companies because they are often outdated as soon as they're written. But I will mention a few kinds of research tools that I recommend and a couple that I use frequently.

You need a powerful, business database that aggregates information from a wide variety of reputable sources. For tools that include companies from multiple industries, my current favorite corporate research tool is *Avention (avention.com)*. With this service your scouts can discover a wealth of up-to-date, relevant information about your global accounts. You'll find all of the corporate persona information plus individual contacts, SWOT analysis (Strengths, Weaknesses, Opportunities, Threats) for the largest companies, industry information, competitors, financial data, a detailed dossier, sales conversation ideas, and the ability to track news updates and whale signs.

Avention integrates with salesforce.com, which is an important point if that is your CRM. You can also find excellent resources in the academic versions of *LexisNexis (lexisnexis.com)* and *Hoovers (hoovers. com)*, which are powerful business databases, in your local public or collegiate library.

Circulate information into the hands and minds of your sales and account management teams and keep the flow of customer information moving constantly throughout key areas of your company, like a spiral that keeps growing as more information is shared in multiple directions.

In addition to research tools, you need communication tools to put the right information in the right place for the right people at the right time. One of course is your CRM. The other is a strategic account management system designed for large, complex accounts with multiple engagements, such as the global accounts I'm talking about. I like *Revegy (Revegy.com)*, which also can be seamlessly integrated with your CRM. I'll talk more about account management tools later when we discuss the sales process, but I mention them here because they are fundamental to a customer knowledge perspective.

Communication

When a scout has gathered and organized a rich set of information, historic and current, about a global company and all the components of its persona, whether it's stored in a database or circulated in a series of reports or whatever, the scout will have learned a great deal. But the sales team and other subject matter experts will not yet have learned anything. To them, the material is just information.

Information only becomes knowledge when an active mind engages with it—by reading, watching, listening, discussing, debating, reviewing, comparing, contrasting, questioning. The scout's work is useless unless your team is deeply committed to sharpening their saw through this kind of study. It is just as important—probably much more important—as deep knowledge of your product and value proposition.

Company executives and sales leaders should be determined to make customer knowledge a core cultural capability.

WHALE HUNTING TIPS FOR KNOWING

Knowledge. There is no substitute for acquiring deep knowledge, over time, about your most important customers. Determine whether your research function for global accounts is a marketing or sales support service and put someone in charge. In The Whale Hunters' Process™, the salesperson does not typically conduct the basic research, but everyone on the team is responsible for learning what's been discovered.

Research. Use a wide variety of traditional and social media research sources—company websites and blogs, your local public or collegiate library, subscription local or cloud-based research databases, corporate and industry analytic reports from major research firms, analysts' reports, SEC filings, the CEO's Quarterly Conference Call, Google searches, LinkedIn connections and relevant LinkedIn groups. Call The Whale Hunters for outsourced research.

Process. Pay consistent attention to the key accounts that you have already or that you are targeting. Develop a seamless process to share information between the researchers and the sales team—this may be your CRM or another shared workspace, a regular conference call or Skype, or a part of each sales meeting.

Communication. Remember that the research works both ways—salespeople should share their new discoveries with marketing to augment what marketing is learning from external sources.

Visit my website at
http://thewhalehunters.com/brainstorm
to download your FREE copy of the

Global Account Team Brainstorm Motivator

Use this worksheet to explore what you know and
what you need to find out about your
key global accounts and their subsidiaries

Use it to coach your team

Help get marketing up to speed

CHAPTER 2

BUSINESS KNOWLEDGE

A customer loyalty research company was growing and had landed some bigger clients than usual. They were typically hired by a marketing director to conduct research about their customers. But they were frustrated in trying to move higher up into the organization, where their research could actually influence strategy and become much more valuable. Here's what we discovered. They employed an exceptional staff of data experts—academic researchers. The same people who conducted the research made the final presentations to the marketing team. The presentation was all about the research—not about how what they learned about customers should fit into a bigger picture. The researchers didn't know much about business; they knew about research. And really, research is a kind of commodity. Only when the company started pairing a researcher with a business development expert for sales and presentations did they break through the value barrier—matching what they had learned to their customers' business issues.

Multinational and global companies have all of the usual business issues as well as issues unique to their global reach. Their size makes them unwieldy. Corporate culture is influenced by all of the national and local cultures under their umbrella. Members of a multi-national senior management team have different standards of proof, different tolerances for risk, and different attitudes toward leadership that they've derived from their home culture. They are deeply immersed in critical business issues all the time.

Unless you can help them solve problems and gain a competitive edge, you are superfluous.

Speed of Business

Gerhard defines what he believes to be the most important issue that is common to all global companies:

> *The first challenge is the speed of business. Global companies are going through an enormous transformation, and they need to not only adjust to the changes in the marketplace in different countries, but also to constantly align their people, process and technology.*
>
> *That is an enormous challenge. When it comes to directing that transformation, you will have to think about the insight they have at the time they make a decision, and you look forward with your headlights to see what's coming on the timeline of innovation. Their decisions are often obsolete, superseded by new innovation by the time they implement what they had decided on. We're in a precarious decade where companies have more big data, with predictive and prescriptive analytics, and we have more tools to make decisions; yet we know that all those great tools have a shelf life.*
>
> —GERHARD GSCHWANDTNER

When Gerhard says "you will have to think about the insight" and "you look forward with your headlights," he directly refers to you. You the salesperson, you the sales manager, you the C-level person whose company has complex global accounts. In order to increase your value to a global company, you cannot simply be selling your company's solutions to what you perceive as a problem or pain to the prospect. You will need to be offering up ideas to your global customers, bringing your ideas of what's on the horizon, what's new and what's possible, to help them make the best decisions.

Tiffani believes that's totally flipped. The customer now has far more power in the deals than makes sellers comfortable because the rate of change in organizations is terrifically fast. They're working internally; they're doing some preliminary investigation; they're talking to some of their trusted network, associations or other businesses like them. They're going to identify how and where they think they can improve their business using technology or process changes and things like that.

They're doing those things internally, outside of the selling cycle that a provider would try to take a buyer through. By the time they reach out, they may actually have some understanding of what it is they're trying to accomplish. It doesn't mean they're 100% correct and there aren't some flaws in their thinking. That's where sales reps can really add value in that phase of the process. If a customer comes and says we know what we want, it may not always be correct.

Your buyers make decisions, but by the time they reach out to implement those decisions their ideas may be obsolete or at least partially outmoded by newer solutions. A sales team needs to be on the lookout for these outmoded beliefs.

Reputation

A significant global issue is the company's reputation. *Forbes* reported research from The Reputation Institute that found that "workplace, governance, citizenship and financial performance" are more important to a company's reputation than their "products, services, and innovation." [Jacquelyn Smith, "The World's Most Reputable Companies," *Forbes*, April 9, 2013]

Is their reputation a matter of high strategic importance to your global customer? Study their website, and news about them, and their public documents to find out. If you provide marketing or public relations services, bring them new ideas about building their global reputation. Or if your services are in the financial arena, focus on methods to bring more meaningful transparency to stakeholders. If you provide any kind of service to remediate a reputation damaging incident—product tampering, recall, regulatory citation—focus on the value you can bring to their reputation before you talk about your solution.

Cultural Differences

In addition to the speed of business, global companies deal with differences in language and culture among their employees and their customers. They have increasing needs for technology solutions to facilitate global communication, share information, support the work of virtual teams, and operate 24/7. If your technology deals with any of those issues, you'll need to approach them with some understanding of how their global presence influences business issues, not with a demo of your product.

As Matt suggests:

> It's important to make sure you understand the local culture, that you understand the unique nature of how to customize product and sales and message and marketing to the local market. You need to have people that are dedicated to that market, especially drawing on people who have experience in that market, can accelerate your learning curve, and make sure you're doing things right from the get go.
>
> —MATT HEINZ

A global company's executive employees need deep knowledge of language and culture around the world, not only to put forward the company's reputation to meet the various criteria for trust in multiple cultures, but also to learn the government rules and the cultural norms for doing business in different countries. Understanding how to do business in one new country doesn't prepare you to be successful in another.

For business leaders in the United States, a key resource to help you learn how to do business in any other country is the U.S. Commercial Service of the U.S. Department of Commerce, the lead federal agency to help promote and develop U.S. exports of products and services. Look for the U.S. Export Assistance Center in your state; it's part of an international network consisting of U.S. Export Assistance Centers across the country and 165 commercial offices in 82 countries. Through this agency you can find a trade mission, attend a workshop on specific opportunities, find partners on other countries, and receive hands-on help for regulations and other export issues. [Commerce website, 12/30/2015]

Greg who comes from Australia, discusses what it's like for him to do business in Japan:

> *Being a foreigner in Japan you've got pluses, and minuses, obviously. I speak the language so that's a huge plus. I read the language as well, which is rare. You have lots of foreigners who can speak, but they're not literate. We take literacy for granted in our native languages. In most Western foreign languages, being able to read is no big deal, but when you get to Chinese, or Japanese, it's a big deal. I am a bit unusual because I can read as well as speak Japanese.*

> *When I'm dealing in business here, I have the advantage of not being Japanese. If I'm Japanese, I'm constricted by how I must behave, and what I can say, and what I can do. Being a foreigner, I am forgiven for being different. They cut me some slack as a foreigner, which means I can push it a bit harder than my Japanese colleagues can push it. I can be a*

bit more direct than they would be able to be direct. I'm also the president so it gives me more respect. Plus, I'm speaking the language. Plus, I can read the language. Plus, I've been there for 30 years. All those things are pluses.

As an Australian, a foreigner, I'm immediately differentiated. As a foreigner, you're going to be remembered. You're going to stand out in the crowd. Meeting you is an unusual experience because Japanese businessmen don't meet that many foreigners, especially one they can speak with in Japanese. Those are all upsides.

The downside I guess is that I'm not Japanese. To some Japanese it's a "clubby" thing. They feel more comfortable with fellow Japanese. I probably won't get as close as a Japanese person would just by nature of not having as many shared experiences, or outlooks they would have amongst themselves. But I find the advantages far outweigh the disadvantages.

—GREG STORY

What is considered to be "polite" varies from one country to the next. As Greg suggests, some people will forgive a foreigner for behaving out of the norm, but not every culture will extend such forgiveness. Greg surrounds himself with a Japanese staff, as well, in order to do excellent business in Japan.

Many issues relate to being a multinational company—internal considerations as well as external ones. How do you get everyone together in a collaborative organization with the amount of diversity that they deal with every day? According to Kirk,

We have many different cultures – Germany, India, China, Brazil – and we have a diverse international leadership team, but that doesn't mean we always operate as a single, global

company. Regions compete. It's healthy and unhealthy at the same time.

We've grown a handful of accounts to a great revenue stream, but replicating this success isn't cookie cutter and it isn't easy. It takes process, collaboration and unified technology to get it done right. You all have to be working from the same playbook and agree to the goal – grow the business. The global business. Global sales are a competitive team sport that requires every region play to the best of its ability.

—KIRK ROBINSON

Global sales models are complex and many times operate differently within each region for good reason. Kirk Robinson's job is "to simplify global accounts" for Ingram Micro through best practices, common ground and ongoing collaboration. It's a challenge Ingram Micro and other global distributors have yet to completely master. Kirk explains:

Two of the biggest hurdles around international or global expansion of an account come down to two basic, yet big questions: Should we, and how are we going to, take this account global? And, who will recognize the revenue and own the account now that it's moved from regional to global?

There are a ton of country-specific considerations including taxes and regulations to take under advisement. And if you don't have a clear process for expanding into new countries and rules of engagement in play around how the company will recognize revenues and distribute profits your new venture will become a battle ground before and if it ever becomes a greenfield.

Being global or simply doing business in other countries is not a decision any company should make on the spot.

Yet, when a long-term client begs the question: "We want to expand from the US to Canada and simultaneously Germany. Can you help?" Some vendors and resellers say yes without hesitation because they have a global distributor within reach. Others take time to weigh the ask against the investment and opportunity at hand.

—KIRK ROBINSON

While your global or soon-to-be global clients wrestle with their strategic business issue, they will influence the directions of your company. In the most immediate way, you need to keep up with their business challenges in order to be valuable suppliers to them. The executives at global companies expect your salespeople to have a deep understanding of their business, their markets, their industry and their challenges. Conversely, they will also challenge your company to become international. This happens first in sales, as your sales and business development operations need to be extended to other countries in which your clients are entering or expanding their business. But soon after, as your sales begin to develop overseas, so do delivery and customer service requirements.

Customers Expanding

It's going to get complicated quickly when an existing customer in your own country begins to ask you for product and service in an international location. As Kirk describes it,

Moving from regional to international to global takes planning and thoughtful execution. For us, global vendor relationships are common and manageable. Where it gets more complicated is at the reseller level. When a reseller wants to, or in many cases is asked to support a client's business out of country or region, that's when the little differences become big differences, legalities rule and the existing relationship

28

between the vendor and reseller is put to the test – are you in or are you out? How can we make this happen?

—KIRK ROBINSON

In comparison to Ingram Micro, ProPharma Group is a small company. Nevertheless, they too deal with multi-billion dollar international clients, and they face similar issues. ProPharma Group has an international line of business in Medical Information, which they have developed overseas with strategic acquisitions. Now they have locations in Europe and Australia as well as in the US, serving all six populated continents, with call center representatives who speak twenty-eight or so languages. I asked Jeff about the other practice areas in his business, areas that aren't specifically international yet:

Many of our best clients are the big multinational drug companies, and they're great clients. Most of our business with them is in the US. We continually try to decide when is the right time to go to other parts of the world, and so far that's just not been the right next thing to do. All that held us back is that other things have been higher priority, which means we forecasted there's going to be a greater return elsewhere. Our current message is, any time a client wants us to go somewhere, we'll go. We just wouldn't go actively market anywhere off shore except for our Medical Information business.

—JEFF HARGROVES

In the case of ProPharma Group, one of its business practices was so ripe for international expansion that they moved quickly and deliberately to develop that component of their business. In other practice areas, they will allow their customers to lead them overseas when the demand arises.

Let's return to Ingram Micro. Obviously, finding their global sales execution is a key business opportunity. But it has many moving parts, as Kirk indicates, one of which is how to manage profitability:

Many companies lack a global P&L. A sales leader will own the regional P&L for what he or she runs, but global isn't theirs alone. When it's a multi-tiered approach, how do we get paid for the value we are bringing? We're spending a lot of time with our tax people and business development people, meeting with resellers around the world, helping them figure out how import/export works, etc. So we are doing all this new work, but we're a distributor on thin margin business and we must ensure we're getting paid across the board for what we do. It's a big challenge.

—KIRK ROBINSON

If you are Ingram Micro, the globalization of your business presents both tactical and strategic challenges, including the need to spend more time with both your vendors and your resellers to solve specific problems and to develop new processes and business rules. Ingram's vendors need to reconsider their authorizations of resellers, or they may lose some business. Ingram's resellers, even small ones, need to consider acquiring international capabilities, or they may disappoint their customers and perhaps lose some business.

In one of her former positions, Valerie was EVP and leader of a sales team selling to global organizations. She tells the story of one account that definitely transformed her company:

I was tasked with developing and leading an industry specific sales team in the high tech vertical. At the time we were selling logistic services serving North America, but for high tech we had to support international supply chains.

We didn't completely understand the industry or its needs. If you're going to be vertically focused, plan and learn in advance! We learned "on the job," maybe 15 years ago. Now of course there's so much industry information online you can more easily prepare.

The high tech vertical was striving for "perfect order," which means from the point of order to destination the right product, right time, right place, right quantity, damage free, right invoice, and right information. Prior to managing global logistics, we did everything ourselves, but now we had to have partners for ocean and air freight. We became "freight forwarders."

—VALERIE BONEBRAKE

Customer Focus

Now if you're a company that does not yet do business with Ingram Micro (or their vendors or their resellers) understanding this specific set of problems that need solutions gives you an edge. Even if you know a little bit about the globalization of a big distributor, if you have products or services that could be helpful to any of the players in this network, now you have a message that any of them might want to hear. You can craft a message that will cut through the clutter and noise of their other messages.

Your message might look like this to Cisco: "I understand that you are trying to solve the problem of your U.S. authorized resellers needing to become authorized to serve their existing customers who are spreading their business outside of the U.S. I have some experience with this issue; could we set an appointment to discuss what you need to accomplish?"

Or your message to any reseller may become, "Your customers seem to be expanding overseas; do they expect you to follow them? Are you confused about the regulations, taxation, and export require-ments of doing business in another country? I'd like to talk with you about how you're planning to learn what you need to know."

Or a message to Ingram Micro, " I read that you are trying to crack the global sales solution, and that right now your team is having to do a lot of extra work that you can't get paid for. I would love to talk with you about some of the alternatives you've considered."

Any of these approaches is better than the usual cold call or unso-licited email that is all about your company and your products or services. It's not that what you sell isn't important. It simply doesn't become important to your customer until much later. Product-centric sales methods absolutely will not work in the global account environment. Only customer-centered activities will help you to be successful.

As you learn more things about the business issues of your global accounts, you will inevitably discover needs for which you don't yet have a solution; you will discover opportunities that they haven't yet realized. These are the ideas that will spark innovation in your company.

Valerie echoes the experience that Kirk is dealing with:

> *The challenge for the seller is how you manage to innovate without hurting your bottom line. Whatever the customer needs, someone else will figure it out if you don't.*

> —VALERIE BONEBRAKE

You are not the only company whose salespeople are talking to your global accounts or prospects. To be successful, you will really need to out-think and out-plan your competition. There are many challenges to keep up with business trends and business model issues in today's global markets. Valerie gives a few examples.

I deal with companies that are production or selling companies and also logistics service providers. On the producer side more and more we are working with them to understand how the supply chain has to perform in order to meet more complex needs.

For example, take a retailer that was selling mainly through stores. Now they have many selling channels and they want to deliver an omni-channel experience providing a consistent customer experience across all channels. This has changed the world of how they work with their partner companies. To put the processes in place we look at all their sales channels and help them develop a logistics network that can deliver on their brand and their consumer promise, and aligns with their corporate strategy.

In the area of shippers and producers who are looking for providers, as in other industries, they want the providers to come to them with proactive solutions. One of the challenges is if they go through the RFQ process, how can they present a better alternative than what the buyer has asked for? They have to comply with the RFP first and then offer alternatives.

Procurement may want an apples-to-apples comparison, or someone else rejects you for noncompliance.

I see clients with a nice portfolio of blue chip clients, but they are not getting share of wallet with them. Their challenge is to keep and grow the business.

—VALERIE BONEBRAKE

Companies all over the world are frustrated with their lack of success in growing business with their current global accounts. I believe that part of the solution is for sales teams to acquire more knowledge of the corporation and its entire business and develop a greater appreciation for its current corporate strategies and how those may influence the roles and responsibilities of anyone in a leadership position.

The nature of our conversation with global customers has to change. We've been talking about solution selling for decades. We were selling devices, but we spun it as a solution. Now, the customer is saying, "No, I actually want an outcome. I don't want to talk about the individual items to get me to that outcome. I want to talk about the outcome."

We can't only give lip service to the customers' expectations; we have to understand, really understand. The speed of business accelerates, and the pain of change increases. The sales team are the ones who have to craft that vision of the outcome and hold it in front of all the many influencers in the buying process.

What global buyers are saying is: we are tired of sellers who are shallow. Who are focused on their products and solutions and what they can do. We want sellers who will help us devise and achieve strategic outcomes.

As you identify the business issues and trends that global companies face, seek out the specific issues and strategic directions of each company with whom you want to build a relationship. You can use that knowledge to have a substantive discussion with business unit or functional area leaders with respect to how their short-term and long-term goals relate to the corporate strategy. And over time, you can build a relationship in which your company's account strategy is well-coordinated with the customer's corporate strategy and functional unit goals.

WHALE HUNTING TIPS FOR BUSINESS ISSUES

Speed. Explore ways to help your customers cope with the speed of business by looking ahead to new ideas that they may not have discovered. Manage the buying process for them.

Exploration. Understand that your customers may not reveal their toughest business issues to you. Take the initiative to uncover them. Read deeply, watch analysts' reports, set Google alerts, and listen to the CEO's quarterly call.

Perspective. Use your position as a knowledgeable "outsider" to bring new perspectives about problems and opportunities.

Innovation. Remember that if you do not invent a new way to meet your customers' needs, someone else will. Encourage your team to bring new problems to the table and to suggest new services. Talk to your R&D people, your product engineers, your customer service reps.

Experience. Draw on your past experience and that of your team to come up with ideas and examples to help with your customers' thinking.

CHAPTER 3

COACH FOR KNOWLEDGE

When my son Ray was in fourth grade, he burst into the house after school one day, all excited. The school was going to have a Science Fair, and he was going to be in it!

"I'm going to build a laser, Mom! I have everything I need except the ruby!"

I had visions of tooling down to Walmart to check on their ruby selection, for I certainly didn't want to dampen his enthusiasm.

He had learned all about lasers and obviously knew what they were made of. But he did not know the price of rubies, so he didn't know enough.

And if I allowed him to proceed, blissfully unaware that there was no ruby in his immediate future, I would only be setting him up for failure.

Sometimes it may seem as though your global sales team has everything it needs except the ruby! No amount of training, or motivation, or admonition seems to get them over the hump. A sale they're predicted to close mysteriously slips away. Multiple sales over time seem to end in "no decision." The buyers' team goes cold and dark. You're in the final three on a bid selection, but your team blows it in the presentation. And you've had this nagging sense all along that they will lose, but either you don't know how to coach them or you don't have a culture in which you confront your real concerns about the outcome when there is still time to make a difference.

The shaman (VP or Head of Global Sales) at a whale hunting company has a critically important role. Working with the rest of the management team, it's the shaman's responsibility to ensure that the global sales organization has everything it needs to be completely focused on the customers. Not on commissions, or who has the better territory, or why marketing is so lame, or any other internal or external issues. Making that happen will require changes over time in your structure, resource allocation, employee expectations, compensation plan, and other areas as well.

But perhaps most important is the sales leaders' responsibility to select, or design, or deliver the kind of sales training that they believe to be most important for their team. Typically, more training is devoted to product knowledge than to customer knowledge. More training is delivered about how to get in the door than on how to have a compelling conversation when a door opens. More training about you and your company and your CRM and your requirements than on your customers.

From Information to Knowledge

I talked a lot in previous chapters about the importance of knowing the whale—acquiring a great deal of information about a global account. That's the first critically important step for global sellers. They also need to learn more as they interact with buyers. But most of all, they need to process the information that they acquire and turn it into knowledge.

Short one-or-two-day sales trainings will have a minimal effect, if any. Research shows that trainees forget most of what they learned shortly after the training. We hope that your global account teams have been practicing and mastering selling competencies since the beginning of their careers. But to learn how to introduce ideas to your customers beyond what they have yet thought of, you need more than solid sales training—you need knowledge and a commitment to wisdom about business, industry, and markets. That kind of learning is in shorter supply. As a sales leader, you will need to supply some of it yourself and also engage your most knowledgeable colleagues throughout the company and the world. And not just sales colleagues—but knowledgeable people from all functional areas of your company.

Valerie talked about training a sales team in China and other distant places while she was in the U.S.:

> We were training the field sales team in place just to recognize an opportunity and make introductions. That yielded some success, but we spent our time with the 20% of the sales team who were open to embracing new services and new ways of selling. It's hard to do, learning not to push a boulder up a hill. It depends whether a person is comfortable going out of what they know well. We always combined travel, wherever we were going, with training and customer visits. You have to leverage your local, national, and global resources depending on the size of the target and your goals.
>
> —VALERIE BONEBRAKE

Most of Valerie's customers were global even when her team was small. So as the sales leader, she had to make the most of the team's expensive travel and extensive reach. Training was always on the agenda.

Can You Coach?

Recent research says that the most successful people are more coachable than all the others. They crave coaching. If you are one of the ones responsible for their success, learn to be a great coach. Take a class—they are readily available. Or if you're not up to that yet, provide your global sellers with a coach who will work with you. Better yet, hire a coach for yourself and a coach for your team.

Lisa had many years' experience as the shaman both at Xerox and IKON. Now, she focuses her energies on helping her clients land what she calls TOP Line Accounts™. She has also established a Sales Executive Mastermind Group in the Pacific Northwest. These are sales leaders who coach each other while Lisa coaches the entire group. I asked her how she manages working with a global account as a small business owner, as a precursor to how she advises her clients:

> First I follow my own advice. I have a wealth of resources: tools and partners that I can bring to the table, if needed, with my global clients. I represent more than a 'single shingle' which my clients appreciate.
>
> My carefully cultivated network of colleagues is a differentiator and therefore a standard component of my proposals to prospective customers. I have a wide network of vetted, world class resources, which has become a great asset. For example, I often ask them, "What is the latest thinking on this?" This helps me to continually bring new ideas to my clients.
>
> —LISA MAGNUSON

Developing the habits of observation and asking questions, then turning that information over in your mind until you have insights, all the while seeking innovative ideas—that kind of ability begins to make you a priceless global account salesperson. If you are the sales team leader, it's even more important to coach your team to develop these talents. As Gerhard says:

This is really a question of mindset of the sales leaders who direct those people to the larger organization. To me, the three pillars of sales success are the right mindset, the right skill-set and the right tool-set.

What is easiest to change is the toolset. It's easy to say, "Well, we're going to use that tool for analytics, we're going to use that tool for prospecting, we're going to use that tool for social media, and we'll use that tool for signatures or for closing." That's easy to do.

The process (skill-set) is a little more difficult, but the most difficult thing is to instill a mindset that is customer-focused, a mindset that is focused on delivering a better performance with each transaction, a mindset of listening to the customer and understanding customers and coming up with better solutions all the time. We talk about innovation; innovation is part of the mindset.

If you don't have any ideas at a rate that matches the idea generation of your competitor, you're going to slip behind.

—GERHARD GSCHWANDTNER

Gerhard is taking us back to his comments about the speed of business. As a global seller or sales leader, you experience that speed with your customer. The entire sales process on a particular deal probably doesn't feel fast when you are trying to move it along, but more often the deal speed is closely related to the speed of new issues, new assignments, or new something else influencing your buyers' attention every day and interfering with your next process step.

And then Gerhard says you need to generate ideas faster than your competitors as well! We're not talking about the R&D department or product development or other formal methods of innovation in your company. We're talking about the ideas that you generate as a sales team—the sellers, the support team, and the sales manager—in your internal meetings and in conversations with your customers.

If the sales team learns how to routinely pass along these ideas to your marketing and product development colleagues, and if marketing and development learn how to accept them and process them effectively, you will be developing an innovation cycle that becomes a key differentiating factor for your company. These are the kinds of ideas that you can bring back to your client contacts, your sponsors and mentors within your global account—ideas that can make their lives easier and make them look good and be good in their positions.

The role of the sales manager of a global accounts team is not just skill-development. It is all about coaching your salespeople to be able to create a vision for the customer and lead the customer to it, all the time recognizing that customers have many ideas of their own about how their buying process should work. This is a delicate dance, and performing it well will take lots of practice.

Whale Hunting is about preparation, timing, patience, and a long-term view. The window of whale hunting for the Inuit lasted only a few weeks; it could not be rushed, but if they missed it a year would go by before they had another opportunity. They had to learn the cadence of the whale. No amount of longing or cajoling or threatening or promising reward could speed up the whale hunt cycle.

Short Term vs. Long Term

Your customers do not have the same cadence as a migrating whale. Although you know it usually takes a long time to close a deal with them, it can be difficult to get a sense of their timing. I believe that although company management gives lip service to thinking of sales over the long term, almost all sales teams and sales managers feel pressure to close more deals faster. This happens end of quarter and end of fiscal year; more often when crises come up. In far too many companies, this impatience, this short-term panic, undermines your team's relationships with their best prospects and their best global accounts.

How can you resolve those disconnects? As the sales leader, it's your job to make the case for the executive team about how to set expectations for your team. Keeping in mind that a global account may include multiple large divisions and subsidiaries—dozens or even hundreds – your biggest global accounts—whatever you may call them—should be off-limits for short-term pushes.

Just Say No

Aside from encouraging and then permitting your global account reps to take time to develop lasting relationships, you should also be instilling a rigorous practice of saying "no" early and often to pursuing certain deals within a global account or deciding which global customer to pursue next.

This is a hard practice to teach into a younger company and to sustain among your sales reps. They are reluctant to say no to whatever seems to be an opportunity and reluctant to create that filter. They would prefer all possible prospects to be left in rather than filtered out.

Therefore, it is a management decision to create the proper targets and focus the sales reps appropriately.

Sales Enablement

The term and the practice of "sales enablement" are au courant, but the term has multiple meanings. I like Brainshark's comprehensive definition: "a systematic approach to increasing sales productivity."

The term also implies that there is a function in the organization with a role to provide "content" information to salespeople at all of the times that they need it while communicating with customers or prospects.

The role of Sales Enablement may be fulfilled by Marketing, Sales, Sales Operations or some related functional area. Matt prefers that marketing take this role as he equates it to campaign management and training:

> *I believe strongly that good marketing organizations today should own the idea of sales enablement. Marketing has a responsibility well beyond delivering a lead to enable the sales team with messages and tools and accelerants to move those deals forward. For example, when marketing does a lead campaign and generates a bunch of leads for sales, it's not good enough to throw those leads over the fence and say "Here you go, have at them."*

> *Part of sales enablement is thinking ahead enough about that campaign to let the sales team know it's coming but also educating them on who it's going to, what they're being offered, why they're responding. Why would someone in this context respond to this and how are you and sales going to continue the conversation that started with that content?*

> *You're reducing friction for the prospect. If you call someone and say "Thanks for downloading the white paper, would you like to see a demo?" that's moving people too far too fast.*

> *Rather, call people and say "Thanks for downloading that white paper. What's going on in your business that compelled you to request that right now?" It's a continuation of the conversation that was a little less explicit, that started in the prospect saying, "I want that."*

I would never expect any organization, sales or otherwise, to just understand how to do that from the get go. In a sales and marketing campaign, part of that campaign is enabling your sales team to have value out of conversations, build rapport and credibility and qualify prospects after the lead has been generated.

—MATT HEINZ

The campaign might not be a random invitation to your company's mailing list. Maybe it's a targeted campaign to certain people that you're trying to reach in one of your global accounts. Or a campaign going to key people in another division or subsidiary company that is part of your global account, but it's still an entire new company to your account team. That could happen with a company like Novartis, for example. If you're successfully working with Novartis on a project that's underway, you might want to position for a similar deal in Sandoz. But nobody in Sandoz knows you yet. A sales enablement campaign could help.

Sid talked about sales enablement in his company:

We have centralized sales enablement and we have enablement leads focused specifically on inside sales and presales enablement globally. Enablement includes everything from new hire training to ongoing training to keep skills current and relevant. We boil it down into 3 areas of enablement: sales skills (prospecting, objection handling, etc.), product knowledge, and productivity tools.

The enablement team is responsible for delivering this content either virtually or in person, and they have a regular cadence for each quarter in each geography. Front-line managers are the critical element in terms of reinforcing the key concepts from training and enablement sessions. They help to make the enablement skills and guidance regular, everyday behaviors and operations with their teams. It's their job to say, "Hey, what were the key concepts that you learned last week in social selling training that resonated with you? How can I help you incorporate these into your daily activities?"

—SID KUMAR

As your company grows, it's likely that you will have both outside and inside salespeople working your global accounts. However they interact with the customer—whether by phone, videoconference, text, face-to-face, or social media—they need similar coaching in order to develop the ability to translate new information into meaningful knowledge to serve the customer.

Just as your customer continues to change and grow, so does your company. A successful company will continue to develop products and services—as Gerhard said, innovate faster than the competitors. Rachel discussed the implications of that evolution for her global sales team:

One of my biggest challenges is how to keep the messaging fresh and make it relevant and bite-sized for your team. Your team is responsible for knowing their customer, but you need to create pathways for them through marketing or sales enablement, so they have short, sharp pieces of information to take their customers along the journey.

And of course your product will continue to change to stay ahead of the market. How do you keep your salespeople effectively trained on your value proposition and your message to the market?

A great example of this is having two distinct product lines obtained through acquisition, and you're used to selling them as two distinct product lines. To get a big deal, you have to imagine how all your product lines come together to create a truly unique and differentiated experience for your customer.

It's hard because most people in a business are in their silos every day executing on their specific goals, but rarely have opportunities to collaborate as a larger team. But selling into a strategic account, you have to have that vision about how it all comes together to deliver this massive benefit and how you can't undo pieces, because the moment that you can undo pieces then you're not selling a big deal anymore. Not only that, but you also have to inspire the customer to believe that the "future state" that you can deliver is critical for their business.

—RACHEL BARGER

Global accounts require many sales capabilities that are less important in more localized or less complex sales situations. All of the experts represented in this book come from a background of large, complex sales. Usually these sales are service-oriented; where products are involved, services are wrapped around them. They are talking about such sales as enterprise IT or logistics or business process outsourcing or compliance services for pharmaceutical manufacturing or management consulting. When these accounts also cross geographic boundaries, the requirements for sellers get higher.

Coach a Collaborative Culture

Of course, it's not only the national cultures that are important in global accounts. The sales leader has a responsibility to impart and to facilitate the development of a healthy corporate culture as well as the culture of the sales division.

I worked a lot in sales management in Sodexo for ten years. I worked with the sales team. I had sales representative that were not only mentored by me but also recruited and trained, because it's important to have a team you can work with. In terms of compatibility, in terms of having the same core values, it's always a good thing to have common ground. It makes a lot easier the communication about the process of selling, of sales management, and so on. When you are thinking about cultural values, about common values of your company, it's important to implement it from the beginning, and to grow together as a team.

—MIRCEA SARAGUT

A fast-growth culture has two primary characteristics: a high level of internal collaboration and a perception that resources are adequate to meet the need. That second point is important. It's not necessary that your company have huge resources in order to take on global sales. But a high degree of transparency about the financial circumstances promotes buy-in from your team. Your employees need to believe that when they bring in lots of big new business, leadership will use some of the new resources to add capacity, not just expect everyone to take on more work.

Moving Parts and People

Another facet of coaching is dealing with the continual movement of people into different roles and places. This happens simultaneously in your own company and in your customers' companies. New people show up at every level of the hierarchy. The ones who leave take critical knowledge with them, and the ones who come in bring a fresh perspective but a missing history.

Gerhard points out that many companies deliberately move their people around in order to take advantage of international diversity among their staff.

What I am observing from the vantage point of where I'm sitting is that there's a constant change. The tenure in those leadership positions is shifting constantly.

I'll give you an example. It's a truly global company represented in a couple hundred different countries with a sales training and communication staff alone of 300 or more. They have a Global Vice President of Sales and then they have regional vice presidents and it's a very complex system. Why? Because they also have a culture where people never stay in place. They want to teach the variety and diversity, and they want to have somebody who is a regional vice president in South America and then all of a sudden becomes Vice President of Sales.

The global head of sales stays in the position for two years and then becomes president of a division. In many companies there's a lot of musical chairs by design. Why? Because they don't want anybody to get too comfortable in any one position and get in a rut and become routine. They want agile people by gaining flexibility in many jobs. That is their secret and they keep growing and becoming more competitive.

The complexity of the VP of Sales Worldwide or the chief revenue officer worldwide is increasing. The management or the organizational structure really depends on who is running that company and what is their tradition, what is their culture. If a company leaves a global VP of sales in the position for too long, it is actually a recipe for long term failure.

This is something that I'm observing in large and successful companies, that you absolutely need to design like you design in products – you design obsolescence. In these

positions, you need to say, you're going to stick with this for
x number of years, and then you move on.

—GERHARD GSCHWANDTNER

In a Whale Hunting village, there was no concept of planned obsolescence. There was, however, a concept of continual learning in a
sort of apprenticeship model. Children began to learn the various
roles as young as four years old, when they first participated in a
harvest. As they grew, their responsibilities increased. The Inuit elders
taught through example, stories, and music.

Applying this industrial product-development tactic to tenure in
high-level sales management jobs in global companies is an interesting model of leadership development. In this case, companies
do not want their sales leaders to become obsolete; rather, they
want them to master successive, high level jobs at a rapid pace. The
many purposes of this strategy include to cross-pollinate global
sales regions, to maintain a fast-paced selling atmosphere where a
VP has to make her numbers quickly in each new position, and to
eliminate some of the problems of global cultures and practices by
providing executives with rapid baptismals into new surroundings.

For everything that might be gained, however, something is lost
among the sales teams in these companies, who must cope with
new leadership every couple of years, and the sales VPs who must
quickly learn to know and to lead entirely new teams.

I asked Matt if he thought it was a good idea to move the VPs every
couple of years, and he put that concept into a broader context:

It's really important for them to spend as much time with
their customers as possible. I would say that includes getting
into local markets and understanding first hand what the
differences are. I worked at a company once where for

several months we did what we called a "customer listening tour." We would take a handful of executives around the country to do dinners and networking events and round tables with customers. Initially we prioritized sending out our customer-facing managers and executives, but what we ended up doing was sending our non-customer-facing employees out to do it.

It was a huge, huge learning opportunity for folks in development, folks in finance, folks who build the product. Suppose you've got a customer team that's always said, "We need this thing." The development team says, "Oh, it's too hard." But they go out and meet clients and all of a sudden the dev team comes back and says, "Holy cow, we need to build this!"

Moving around means living in different areas; I can see the benefit of that. I think more and more it's just continuing a regular touch with the customers. Maintaining a regular heartbeat and pulse of what's going on with your customers, with them individually in their mind, in the context of how they work. That more than anything is the underlying objective.

—MATT HEINZ

Matt offers one more specific example of how to focus on the customer. Take people out, get them to travel, meet with customers at their places and talk about their issues. Your team will grow exponentially in their understanding. Getting more of your people out into new world regions is a powerful part of their continuing education. As Rachel notes:

Get people traveling more. It's really powerful getting product teams out in the field, especially to spend time internationally. Europeans and the Asian customers often get frustrated because visits from headquarters are less typical or sometimes never occur. They also often think their own account managers aren't current or "in the know" as their US counterparts because they're not located in your headquarters. Meeting them on their own turf is critical and a company that has a serious focus on having product, marketing and headquarters executives out in the field can really differentiate, build stronger relationships and better understand their customers.

—RACHEL BARGER

So by moving people around, whether for two-year assignments or two-week visits, you will meet two sets of needs: your customers' need for attention and your team's need for global perspectives and experiences.

Coaching your global sellers really means coaching everyone in your company to know the customers at a level of detail. It's not just marketing saying, "These are the personas," and it's not just sales saying, "Customers come first." It's a deliberate agreement among the entire senior management team that a customer focus means making use of the information to build intelligence among all of your employees. As the sales leader, it's your job to spearhead this kind of attitude and behavior.

WHALE HUNTING TIPS FOR COACHING

Readiness. Be prepared for each session. Work with each member of your team to determine your mutual agenda and move towards it each time.

Clarity. Understand that coaching is different from management. You will still want to meet with your team members to discuss their metrics and progress and to be sure they are on track. This is different from coaching; don't confuse the two roles.

Modeling. Chances are good that you were promoted to a sales leadership position because you proved to be a good salesperson. Although sales management is much different from being the seller, be a good role model of the kind of behavior that you want to encourage on your team.

Support. These will be times during a sales process when you will be with your sales team in front of the client. Prepare your team and yourself well to fulfill the role expected of you, not to usurp their role.

Confidence. Coaching is for those people that you believe in, the ones who are already good and hungry to get better. If you don't believe in someone's capacity to become the kind of team member you need, it is best to make a management decision, not a coaching one.

KNOWLEDGE SUMMARY

The lessons from this chapter are all about the most important element in your sales process—your customer. Many sellers are pursuing large, global accounts, and you will face unprecedented competition as you move up and around in that space. I'll delve deeper into relationships with your customers as we drill down into more specific parts of your sales strategy. For now, the key point is to get your customer at the forefront of your thinking and acting. And embed that concept into the hearts and minds of your team.

To demonstrate unmatched knowledge of your customer's organization, industry, market, business issues, and expectations will become a priceless way to differentiate from your competitors. Do you think everyone else is already doing that? Well, talk is cheap. A dedicated customer focus is not the norm.

PART II

STRUCTURE: GET ORGANIZED

WHALE HUNTING PERSPECTIVES

Whale Hunting begins with clarity of roles, responsibilities, and rewards. In the Inuit village, some people prepared the equipment while some sewed the clothing, others scouted the whales, still others paddled the boat out into the sea, and others gathered tools and waited on shore to help with the harvest. It was a carefully organized activity, right down to the seating assignments in the sealskin boat, where the harpooner sat in the front and the shaman in the rear. Everyone contributed, and everyone shared in the rewards according to their contributions.

But it was all about the whales.

The Inuit teams' success depended upon being ready for the whales. The whales came at their own pace in their own time. If the hunters missed the short window of opportunity, there were no more whales for a year.

Likewise, in modern companies, the hunt with global accounts must be carefully orchestrated with roles, responsibilities and rewards made clear. As your company grows, you will need to adapt your sales structure to better meet the needs and desires of your customers.

While your company is still small with only one or two salespeople, you don't have much to decide. But if you're intent on fast growth, you need a plan for how to organize your sales functions as you grow and when you are much, much bigger.

Territories and channels, inside and outside distinctions, sales methods and models, seller roles, resellers, sizes of your customer companies and more figure into the organizing mix.

How many times will you reorganize your sales structure as your company grows and you take on bigger accounts? Perhaps more than you know. If you are paying attention to the needs of your customers, you will probably find yourself on some kind of path that leads to greater specialization because you want your most knowledgeable people leading the team to work with each whale.

Within the organizational structure, how you allocate sales personnel is especially important. If you want some people to open doors and others to grow an existing account, make that clear. If you want the sales people only to hunt and close deals, provide them support for administrative tasks.

A critically important component of your structure is how the sales organization interacts with marketing. Far too often I find sales and marketing at odds with each other or living in different universes. But the most successful teams have a close and vigorous collaboration, an almost seamless integration.

Just like the Inuit whale hunters, modern whale hunters deploy their resources strategically.

The focus of this section is the organization of your global account sales operation—the structure, the allocation of personnel, and the relationship with marketing.

CHAPTER 4

A GLOBAL ECOSYSTEM

I visited a large inside sales call center of a global technology company. The SVP of sales sent me there to learn why there was so much turnover among the sales staff, why they were not successful at selling bigger deals, and to design some training to fix the problem. I interviewed sales managers and sales people with various terms of seniority. We talked about hiring practices, management styles, quotas, work load, lead generation, and many other characteristics of their work.

But the kicker came from a successful and hard-working young saleswoman, who said, "I am successful at building a relationship with my customers and I make a lot of follow-up sales and new sales to the same people. But whenever my total sales to one customer reach a certain point, they take that account away from me and hand it to a regional guy. Suddenly the account's too big for me to handle!" She told me she would be moving on to a new company at her first opportunity.

Everyone knew that's how the sales process worked—and how the people in charge distinguished between a "call center account" or a "named account" that was handled only in the field. But management couldn't figure out that no amount of training could fix that problem of incentives.

The sales organization in my story was not structured to motivate an individual sales person to grow her accounts—in fact, it was counter-productive to that goal. As a result, the best salespeople in the inside sales group, rarely promoted, were motivated to find a better opportunity with a different company.

Likewise, this sales organization was not organized to please loyal customers. The woman in my story went out of her way to provide excellent service to her customers. She followed up on the delivery of every order and did all kinds of trouble-shooting to fix any kind of mistakes. She kept her customers informed of everything that was new, or anything that was on sale, and she brought them ideas on how to grow their own business. In short, she built positive, powerful relationships with her customers. But when their business reached a certain level, she could no longer serve them. In fact, she was not even allowed to conduct the handoff or explain it. Whether they liked it or not, suddenly they had a new rep, someone with a perceived bigger job or more important job—that is, more important in the eyes of the selling company.

Your Organizational Purpose

So, if they weren't organized to encourage salespeople to excel, and they weren't organized to reward customers for their loyalty, what purpose did their sales structure fulfill? What were they organized to accomplish? They were only organized to separate inside sales from field sales, or small account sellers from large account sellers. In other words, to suit themselves. And it wasn't working, and they knew it! But still the reasons eluded them.

If you are a large company, your global account structure may have been put into place some time ago, and it will be difficult to change. And if you are a small or midsize company, chances are you will start doing business with a global account obliquely rather than with a deliberate strategic decision. You are doing business with a local division of a multinational company, and suddenly you have an opportunity to do an international deal with them. Or you are doing business with a local company that one day opens an overseas location and asks you to supply them in their new location as well. Or you could be a start-up with a global strategy from the outset. Whatever your circumstance, the question is the same: "How are we going to organize our sales force to go after global accounts?"

Typically, when companies discuss organizational structures and possible reorganizations, they are inwardly focused—thinking about what makes most sense from a cost perspective, a management perspective and a capacity perspective. Looking at these decisions from a customer perspective may give you different answers as well as new ideas. Decisions about the sales team structure relate to equally important decisions about other business functions. How will you become superior to your competitors in how you approach your customers and prospective customers in all facets of the business?

Consider Options Early

Changing your organizational structure is hard and painful. You will disrupt employees' work patterns, their customers, their colleagues, managers, and maybe even their families. You will probably change their compensation and incentive package. People will perceive themselves to be winners or losers in a reorganization, and morale may suffer. Even the "winners" will have a steep learning curve and will experience the loss of familiarity and relationships into which they have invested time and energy. Even more important, changing your structure will disrupt your customers' expectations of your company and relationships with your people.

Therefore, it is important to think through your options before you make a decision. When your company is small, you cannot operate in the same way as a large company. But as close as you can come to where you hope to be, ideally, when you are larger, the easier the growth process will be for you, your employees, and your customers.

Outside or Inside

Multiple models and many variations are possible for global account sales, but not every model will be most beneficial to your customers or cost-effective for your stage of growth.

A common pattern is to begin with a field-based or "direct" or "outside" team, organizing salespeople into regions, and eventually breaking down large regions into smaller regions. A regional type of organization means that each sales rep has a territory within which he or she is responsible for opening doors for sales to new customers as well as making new sales to existing customers. The expectation is that the salespeople will often call on customers face-to-face at the customer's location.

A territorial sales structure can become problematic and result in deals being lost because the most knowledgeable person for a particular deal is in another territory focusing on other accounts. Or the deal requires the expertise of an industry team, but you don't really have one. Or a sales person wants to pursue a global account with a global strategy but doesn't know how because many of its locations are in territories assigned to other people. Or your regional sales person is compensated primarily for opening new doors, bringing on new logos, and therefore pays less attention to gaining new business from existing customers.

If your customer's territory is global, how can you limit the territory of the sales team responsible for that customer or prospect? Or if a customer grows into a global presence that you did not anticipate, can a regional model serve them properly?

The answer is most often no.

Instead of field-based salespeople organized by territory, a totally different method is to start with an inside sales model, as Sid explains:

With the buyer's journey becoming more and more digital, many organizations are building inside sales teams to begin engaging with prospects earlier and more often in the sales cycle. For some organizations, the only go-to-market model – at least initially – is inside sales. As they start to move up into the enterprise, they start to build out their direct sales forces. There could be a good period of five to seven years where you don't even have a direct sales force and you're doing everything inside. Inside sales is really about two things – cost and coverage – which are especially important early on in an organization's life cycle.

—SID KUMAR

Starting out with an inside sales team makes real sense, particularly for software companies, when you intend to do business with multi-national or global customers. Your team is not limited by geography, you don't incur travel costs and time on travel, and you can recruit sales employees who have regional cultural language and knowledge. As you grow, you can place inside sales professionals in various regions around the world.

But inside sales is not only a strategy to get started with more coverage for less money; it's a way to align with your customers' preferences:

Inside sales is going to play an increasingly bigger role in go-to-market coverage models from my perspective. You see what's happening to the buyer's journey – prospects want to engage digitally, and they want to engage when and how they want to do their upfront research. The explosion of inside sales over the past 5 years is directly correlated with the proliferation of mobile devices and the ready and constant access to digital assets made possible by the Internet. To be successful during this paradigm shift, it will be critical to

63

align your go-to-market model with how customers want to
buy from you. We recently rebranded our inside sales team
to 'digital sales' to reflect this new market reality.

—SID KUMAR

Sid provides an example of organizing according to the wishes of the customer. There is a lot of lip service to that concept, but I find it hard to identify real examples of companies actually listening to their customers and then organizing the sales team deliberately around the customers' preferences. Looking at data and trends will help you decide. Talking with your customers and your closest prospects will be even better. When do they want to see someone in person, when do they prefer the phone or Skype or email or a web meeting? What methods do they use internally to keep a distributed team on the same page? Find out, and let their preferences dictate how you serve them.

Complications

So far we've looked at two sort of opposite strategies—starting out with an entire field-based team organized by territories or starting out with an entirely inside sales team, organized by territories or some other pattern. But this book is not really about starting up a sales team—it's about structuring a sales team to go after global accounts. Strategizing around how to organize your sales operation is hard enough for accounts that reside in your own country, or are headquartered even in your own region or territory. But when you look at large global accounts, it's a completely different operation. In fact, it seems to have little in common with more localized accounts, even if they are large.

The territory model becomes problematic once you are doing business with a headquarters location or major subsidiary of a global corporation. If you want to increase your business with that customer, you will need a sales presence, and a service and delivery presence, in multiple locations around the world. The inside sales model becomes problematic when you want to sell enterprise deals, which almost always require a considerable live, onsite presence in order to close them and then, of course, to deliver.

There is a natural movement from regional structures to industry verticals because the global customers expect sellers to possess a great deal of industry knowledge. You could, for example, begin your global account outreach only with a single vertical, and later expand to another vertical if that makes sense. If you sell into many vertical markets, however, Matt suggests that you expand by geographic territories first, in order to master each local market along the way:

> I highly recommend companies look at creating geographic territories versus vertical territories as you are getting started with localization and as you mature in your distribution in sales and markets around the world. As your organization gets smarter and is able to train new people more effectively on the way that you've translated your business, your product, your efforts into a local market, then you can say "We're going to have someone that owns healthcare, and they're going to have healthcare among multiple markets and multiple local areas."
>
> —MATT HEINZ

You can't underestimate the need for local knowledge—as Matt calls it "translation" of all your stuff into one market at a time.

Company Examples

It's instructive to look at midsize companies that are already serving global clients to see the kinds of decisions they have to make about structuring their sales force. ProPharma Group is a rapidly – growing company that serves a single industry cluster—pharmaceuticals, biotechnology, and medical devices. However, they have eight different practice areas. They are finding it challenging to develop the appropriate structures for their sales and business development operations as they grow. Jeff explains:

> We're currently organized for our consulting practices with a regional structure in the U.S. Beyond the regional salespersons, we have two account managers who are each responsible for growing five or six accounts. Each of those accounts is a multinational drug firm with multiple sites in the U.S. and abroad. The salespersons are tasked with growing those key accounts wherever they can grow them. Accounts will preferably be in multiple different areas and with multiple different practices, but at this point, we're only holding them accountable for the total dollar amount of the sum of their assigned accounts.

> —JEFF HARGROVES

The first decision ProPharma made was to assign specific salespersons to key global accounts. For now, how they grow those accounts is up to them. They may come up with a multi-country project, or a project in another country, or they may sell entirely into U.S. locations for now. Jeff continues:

> We do have one practice-specific salesperson attached to our medical information business. But we're adding two more so that the current person will be focused just on the Eastern U.S. We'll have one new person focused on the Western U.S., and one new person focused in Europe. That will be three people focused on that one practice.

> There's the sales side and then the operational side. On the sales side, we're just continuing to try to make the right decisions about where to have the salespeople in the global capacity. We will next look to and make the decision for

whether we need to add someone in Asia Pacific, and if they're going to cover that region, should they be located at Australia, should they be located in Hong Kong or Singapore? Trying to make those decisions but also to balance that with the other side of the equation – we really have to build it out operationally even before we can go sell it. This is not the type of business that you can sell and then figure it out. We won't be able to win work unless we can convince the client that we've already got the abilities sitting there.

—JEFF HARGROVES

They are facing the problem around growth that every company faces: how to manage increasing costs as they move ahead, how to finance essential investments without excessive risk.

We talk about all of the different options of how to configure the sales organization. We think we may be able to benefit from having more than two account-dedicated salespeople. And we think our account managers may be overstretched with five accounts – that they might be able to get a better return by focusing on even fewer key accounts.

—JEFF HARGROVES

Jeff's company is growing fast through increasing sales and strategic acquisitions. The accelerated growth keeps the sales functions in a continual state of flux, requiring constant attention and reconsideration. People dedicated to specific accounts, people dedicated to product lines or business units, people dedicated to territories—you may need all of those.

Lisa provides insights on some of the organizational challenges that her customers face and how they resolve them. Lisa's clients range from Fortune 50 – Ricoh USA has been her client for 10 years – to smaller companies with a single sales team and all sizes of companies in between. They have two things in common: they are selling to large companies and they are focused on the top line. Her clients are pursuing companies like United Health Care, Novartis, and Amazon, to name a few, which will give you an idea of the size of customers that they are dealing with.

As I work with my clients who have a global focus, they tend to consider resources, both sales and support resources first and foremost. As an example, a mid size company may want to pursue a global prospect, but they may be constrained by the resources within their organization. Needed resources include traditional sales and sales support roles but also administrative, legal, financial, technical, R&D, marketing and other critical functions. It's important to do an in-depth analysis of the opportunity and the risk before deciding to mobilize the full account team that will be required to land a global contract.

For example, in one midsize company that I work with, a global customer is asking for them to place people on site through the contract—a technical account manager and perhaps a customer service employee. This is a real differentiator and an opportunity to solidify the contract for years to come. My client is getting to know their customer's business with an eye towards differentiation. If you embed people, it's hard for that customer to make a change down the road. As the account grows, management may make them a distinct team; taking customization beyond a global or industry focus to an actual customer team (i.e. The IBM Team or The Oracle Team). I also encourage my clients to watch for trends with their customers. We're thinking from the customer's perspective – What are their roadblocks? Where are they frustrated? What opportunities do they see for improvement? The account team can then consider

how they can use the insights gained to build a long-term,
mutually beneficial relationship.

—LISA MAGNUSON

From another perspective of a small company making a big global move, Valerie tells the story of how in her former position as Executive VP in a global logistics company, she began opening business operations in China. Valerie's experience confirms that sales and delivery have to grow up in tandem when your company begins to expand its business to a new country:

> *We had an existing freight forwarding service, but we didn't*
> *have offices in China. First we made a strategic acquisition*
> *and then we established a joint venture with a state-owned*
> *enterprise. Next we planned a continent-by-continent*
> *rollout. Our sales were highly dependent upon our sister*
> *company in the U.S., which had long-time relationships*
> *for national freight. We had people on the ground to deal*
> *with their local counterparts for a big consumer products*
> *company manufacturing in China. Local offices worked*
> *with the customer at origin. We had a small global sales*
> *team, including a liaison to our U.S. team. This person was*
> *responsible for the ongoing education of the U.S. team, which*
> *was organized to support local and national customers.*

—VALERIE BONEBRAKE

Valerie's example illustrates the value of defining the work that needs to be done and parceling it out imaginatively. Partners, joint ventures, people with multiple responsibilities. The structuring alone of the global sales teams becomes complicated, regardless of the size of your company. It is clear that no particular structure organizes a global sales team better than all others. It's always a matter of what will help you do the best job for your customers while managing your costs and growth strategy. As your customers grow and as your deals with them grow, changes in structure may be required from time to time. You may organize differently for different customers depending upon their preferences and expectations.

Hari described one such plan that has proven appropriate as he advises clients:

> Going global can't be making a splash at every single client in the whole world, which is reaching to 51,000 companies and saying, "Hey look, I'm global and I'm coming for you." That's unaffordable. You just can't do that. Especially, if you're a new company and you're going from a local to a global market. There's an art of managing the growth at the same time making sure that the growth comes at a pace with profitability. Even if it's not extremely profitable, at least it should not be value dilutive and should not eat into existing profits. You need to make some investments, for example set up shop in China, if you want to sell in China, but look at baby steps before getting in there and establishing a full-fledged army.

> —HARI SHANKARANARAYANAN

The companies that are doing this successfully calculate their costs and potential ROI in advance. Just as you wouldn't expand your national reach by going east coast and west coast at the same time, go to one place that makes sense for you and start out safely. Hari continues:

> A lot of people tend to believe it's a chicken and egg; until you have the army of sales people you won't really be able to grow, and until you grow you can't afford the army of sales people. There is a fine balance, and you need to understand the balance of how to get the sales team and win some business before you set up the local services teams. If there was one point I could say that successful companies have

done is that they have not really developed any delivery teams in a local environment unless they had a fairly large presence of clients in that geography.

—HARI SHANKARANARAYANAN

Sell first and deliver however you need to do that before you make a big investment in locating services in the new country. If you have a new customer in China, to deliver on that deal will probably be expensive. You may have to send people there or pay others to help. Later on, you can bring down the cost by setting up shop in that country where you have multiple customers. Here's more from Hari:

You will come to a place like Singapore or Hong Kong and set up a shop only selling. Many times companies will choose to do that with partners. Look for a like-minded partner, maybe a company that is used to delivering similar products or services but they aren't really in the space that you offer. That can be another avenue to open a few doors. Once you open a few doors, get a sales person in there.

When you've closed a few deals and have a steady revenue stream coming in, set up a delivery team there as well, which could be more localized. Until then everyone will be flying out from North America to Asia for delivering or selling. Franchising, setting up sales partners or channel partners, taking baby steps toward selling globally are some things that companies have done in the past.

—HARI SHANKARANARAYANAN

Selling through Channels

Another sales organization strategy involves enlisting partners, resellers or independent representatives to sell your products to the end users. They may be called Value-Added Resellers (VARs), dealers, distributors (who sell to resellers) or partners—but collectively they are referred to as channels or "the channel."

What's important here is the growth and expansion of that model. Tiffani offers a detailed explanation of how the global business environment is driving the need for channels. As she says,

> *There is no vendor, no matter how big, that can deliver an end to end solution globally, especially as customers are looking to digitally transform. Even if you're a smaller organization with only 100 employees and 10 offices with 10 people in each of them around the world, you would have the same problem as if you're GE. Because you still have a global problem; you're still in 10 counties. Whether it's 10 people or 10,000 people, you need someone to make sure that your business runs 24/7.*
>
> *One of the biggest challenges for vendors, providers and manufacturers is that there has to be a way in which they can gain scale in a cost effective manner. The best way to do this is by using "third party companies" such as value added resellers, system integrators and managed service providers. These partners are able to augment a vendor's sales and account coverage models, provide system integration and implementation services and perform ongoing support and maintenance services. The power of that ecosystem I believe will be the competitive differentiator going forward.*
>
> —TIFFANI BOVA

So there's not one channel; there's a channel methodology. An ecosystem point of view. What could a channel look like for your company? If you were to position yourself as the hub of a global enterprise supported by third-party companies, what might the third parties do? Would they be your sales team, or part of it? Distribution? Customer service? Installations?

It makes sense to explore channels as early as possible in your global sales reach. A channel can help you get started as well as take you to scale.

The best way to organize is the way that makes life easiest for your customers. Whatever the size of your company, your global customers do business 24/7 everywhere in the world. Positioning your company inside of a powerful ecosystem is one key to your competitive advantage.

WHALE HUNTING TIPS FOR ECOSYSTEM

Focus. You will make the best decisions about the structure of your sales organization if you remain fiercely customer-focused.

Differentiation. As your company grows, make deliberate decisions about how to organize your sales team to meet the needs of global customers. Work towards a structural plan that will best make a visible difference to your customers.

Planning. Consider how you may eventually need to reorganize installation, services, and customer service functions as well as your sales functions. Plan so that you are not required to make multiple, costly changes in structure as your company grows.

Ecosystem. Look at your company from the point of view of its position within a global ecosystem. How could you best fit, and what support would you need, to serve your customers all the time, anywhere in the world.

Reorganization. Don't assume that your organizational structure is fixed in place. Rather, be willing to reconsider from time to time as you are growing. It's a big mistake to hang on to a dysfunctional structure long after it has outlived its usefulness.

CHAPTER 5

PLACE YOUR PEOPLE

The international sales team of a fast-growing technology company convened in a southwest USA resort city for an annual meeting. Their somewhat unknown company was selling enterprise software to some of the world's largest companies.

I was invited to lead a one-day workshop on large-account selling with their Asia Pacific team. The sales leadership was committed to a team selling process, with sales support people collaborating with the sales reps at every turn, and they all wanted to learn how to become even more effective.

But their first issue was that sales support people were not invited to the sales convention, even though it was to be focused on training, learning, and new ideas for success. To their credit, the APAC leaders said none of them would come unless they all came; management relented, and their teams came together.

Nevertheless, this lavish convention, celebrating sales success, focused entirely on rewarding the rock-star sales guys. The guy with the best year was given a new sports car. The top 50 or so were going on a cruise with their spouses. No team awards; no team recognition. Sales engineers, pre-sales specialists, account managers need not apply.

Once you have made the decision to be a whale-hunting company—to deliberately go after bigger companies for deals ten or twenty times or more the size of your current deals—you need to decide whether all of your current salespeople will hunt much bigger accounts as well as regular-sized deals or if whale hunting will be a specialty. The larger you grow, I believe the more you will want whale hunting to be a specific component of your sales structure, with its own goals and its own sales practices.

As you are growing it's important not to let the idea take hold that the people who sell big accounts are much more important than those who sell smaller accounts or those who become account managers. Over time, with more whale hunting you're likely to have more big accounts and fewer small accounts. But whatever the mix, the sale of all of the kinds of accounts that you need should get equal recognition—not only whale sales.

On the other hand, working with global accounts requires highly developed knowledge, skills, experiences, and points of view, so it's important not to put anyone in that role just because of their seniority or their current territory. You can't afford to put the wrong people on a whale hunting team. The hunt is too expensive and too important.

A critical structural decision is how to organize your sales people—do you envision different sales roles, with different functional responsibilities and different skill sets? Inside people and field sellers? New product specialists? That's what this chapter is about—how to allocate your people who will be hunting whales.

Hunters and Farmers

I was frankly surprised to hear so much about "hunters" and "farmers", given that many sales commentators deem that to be an outmoded distinction. "Hunters" refers to the salespeople who bring in new deals with new customers; "farmers" are the account managers who handle everything else after the initial sale.

To some degree, these monikers came from the outside/inside sales dichotomy—inside salespeople being considered farmers, while the outside team were the hunters. In this old world of sales, hunters looked down their noses at farmers. In a sense, everyone did. The high energy, high-powered, highly-commissioned, well-traveled hunter was considered to be superior to the steady, low-key, desk-bound farmer when it came to how the company made money. In fact, I would argue that even today, "hunters" are believed to be more valuable and in shorter supply than farmers. It's far from true, but it's a persistent myth!

Many of the farmers who used to keep their company's customers supplied with endless refills and re-orders can no longer earn their keep in the same way. The B2B consumer no longer buys in that way. The purely commoditized purchases belong to a procurement organization, or a procurement division, or a completely outsourced procurement service.

Even more sophisticated buying decisions such as consulting services or engineering support or business processes are being outsourced to a procurement vendor with a software solution or an uber-consultant who hires and manages all of the other outsourced services.

Changing Roles

Where the terminology of hunters and farmers still exists, as it does in many global sales organizations, the definitions of these roles have changed dramatically. In fact, it's the farmer's role that has expanded and taken on much greater responsibility and accountability.

I asked Melissa if the terminology of hunter and farmer comes up in her organization:

Yes. I have used it, but to a large degree it is more important to identify the role and determine the needed skill set. It takes a different set of skills to remain successful in one account, nurture it, manage it and continue to find new opportunities. A more consultative approach is required to farm an existing environment versus the more opportunistic approach of finding a new customer or new opportunity. We have both in our organization.

Most companies I have worked for typically employ a few folks referred to as the big elephant hunter – the person tasked with securing a footprint within some of the really large accounts. The remaining sales organization typically will have a set group of accounts and their job is to manage, nurture and look for new opportunities within their existing account base.

—MELISSA DONNELLY

The role of the account manager—the farmer—is complex as Melissa explains. It includes managing, nurturing, and finding new opportunities. In my experience, account managers in service industries almost always get more bogged down in managing current services than they do in finding and working with new opportunities. If the new opportunity is close to where they are already working—in the same division or location, for example—it is more likely to be pursued. But to actively create opportunities in diverse parts of a global account requires a focused team.

Selling new business into an existing global account can be just as hard as opening a "net-new logo." In fact, it can be harder because the customer has pegged your company as a particular kind of provider and may find it difficult to think of you for a wider range of services or a bigger role.

Lisa thinks that whether or not you separate hunter and farmer functions can be a matter of company size. In fact, she points out that there are many aspects of the two positions which are similar, such as the need for strategic account planning,

> From a strategic account planning perspective, 80% of what you do for an existing account is the same as what's needed to land a new account. If you're dealing with global prospects or customers, both require careful and methodical strategic planning that includes architecting goals, strategies, relationship maps and more. Big companies have the resources to implement a hunter/farmer model if they deem it appropriate; many small companies don't. However, whether you want to secure or maintain critical customers, regardless of the sales type assigned, companies should put a high priority on putting the strategic framework in place for all global accounts.
>
> —LISA MAGNUSON

For company size to be the differentiating factor suggests that companies go through a decision-making process as they grow, and once they have the capacity to organize into hunters and farmers, they will choose to do so. Lisa's point is critical: you need a "strategic framework" for global accounts.

Many big companies today have their large account sales organization strictly divided into hunters and farmers. Once you were to buy a software solution or a product solution from a hunter or a hunter team, they would have a way to hand you off to a farmer team to manage the process of serving you and selling new products.

Here's how Melissa explains it:

> I think there's a finite set of activities that need to take place to be successful in selling and managing accounts. The question is, how do you distribute those tasks properly? I've worked

with some organizations where the sales executive owns the entire relationship including the management of product issues, service issues, or whatever else the customer needs.

In these instances, they typically carry between three and five accounts depending upon the size and complexity of the account. It is difficult to say if that's the right mix as the job sometimes requires a more opportunistic approach. Not every account is going to be in the same buying cycle or have the same priorities. You have to provide your salespeople enough opportunity to assure they can make a living, be happy and be successful. Conversely you can't give them so much that you kill them. It's a tough balance and an ongoing struggle.

Where the account manager has fewer accounts, their job is not only to nurture and take care of the accounts to maintain customer satisfaction but also to develop new opportunities. Honestly, I think that might be the harder job.

—MELISSA DONNELLY

Account Managers

If you're not careful starting out, you may hire a team of hunters and then find them becoming so bogged down in customer service that they have insufficient time to open new accounts; then they and you will be dissatisfied. That's when companies turn to an account manager plan, with the account manager responsible for new sales to existing customers. As you get into these role distinctions, the problem becomes in a global account, selling new business is much more like opening doors into a brand new account than simply taking repeat orders from an existing customer. Plus, the seller/account manager embedded in an account has to take on huge responsibilities that are product, service, and installation issues rather than "sales" issues.

Rachel is responsible for global account management in a newer, younger company, and her organization is handling the personnel allocation differently. When new sales need to happen in a global account, the hunters come back in:

> *My account management team are the farmers. We do have a double-up methodology where there is a farmer and a hunter on each one of the accounts, but the farmer is responsible for growing the demand, increasing usage and the day-to-day engagement and identifying the buying signals. In most cases once an opportunity is identified and nurtured the hunters come in at the end and help with the team approach of closing the deal. I think this approach is really important because it helps us scale our sales team and allows the hunters to spend the majority of their time focused on bringing in new logos, but also leverages their expertise closing deals in expansion sales.*
>
> *The ideal scenario is that the hunters are off largely working new logo accounts, and spending a relatively small portion of their time participating on strategic account planning and key customer relationship meetings, but the farmer is really leading that charge. At the beginning it can be a little bit difficult for everyone to understand and embrace their new roles and understand who should take the lead in various stages. Through the course of our first year in this concept we have seen some really effective teams form where both hunter and farmer have well exceeded quota and actually see themselves as a sales unit. I'm interested to see as we evolve if we will keep both a hunter and a farmer on the account or if we will just have farmers and hunters in separate roles.*
>
> *For the hunter and farmer teams that are most effective, getting to know each other well has been the critical success factor. Some of these teams have really achieved a lot of*

traction. It's hard for some, with egos and people who are used to being the quote-unquote "owner" of the account, but I think that the pragmatic ones form the best teams, because they both understand their role, they don't have an ego about it, and they share responsibility. Their approach is then really validated when they start seeing success and start feeling that they are accomplishing more than what they could have done alone. I love triangulating an account, when you have multiple roles and levels mapped and are bringing in the executive sponsor at the right stage – you can't sign big deals without having everybody playing a different role.

—RACHEL BARGER

In many global accounts, such as the ones Rachel describes, the farmer, or account manager, does not behave merely as an order-taker; rather he or she is a true account leader whose job it is to create an organization just for that customer. Their company treats them like a CEO of that account, allocating resource spends and investments as well as sales, and measuring profit and loss for that customer. In that case, an account manager behaves like an entrepreneur whose job it is to bring to the table whatever that customer needs, at any time.

That's how Hari describes his role:

When you work with really large clients that you bet on for a long term association and a continuous flow of revenues, you need to invest in relationships. At each of those clients, you'd need a focused leader architecting relationships and bringing your entire arsenal of offerings to the client.

The responsibility of that leader is to bring the best of your company to the client at the right point of time so that the client can understand the value proposition and buy your services.

Depending on the revenue from the client, you would have either one lead at each client or have a single lead managing multiple clients.

—HARI SHANKARANARAYANAN

For the farmer to act as an entrepreneur, a CEO responsible for the global accounts, is a far cry from the outmoded definition that I introduced above.

I asked my experts, when you differentiate between hunters and farmers, if you have a hunter that has opened the door into a new multinational company and they have made a big sale, if you were to bring a completely different product or service of yours into that company, or you were to pursue an opportunity in a different division, would that still be considered as new or would that go to the farmers? Typically, the farmers are getting renewals and making sure that everything is going along properly. They may be selling that same service into a different division or different part of the company. Are they also trying to sell new services or new products or would you go back to your hunters for that?

In most cases, the farmer is 100% responsible for new sales to an existing account. This is a critical reason for failure to sell as much new business to the current global accounts. Catering to an existing customer, managing deals that you've already sold, usually takes up so much time that little time is left to pursue additional opportunities, especially to develop new opportunities. You leave money on the table.

Cultural Considerations

The differentiation of sales roles makes less sense in an Asia/Pacific region or in some parts of Europe. They are significantly high relationship-centric cultures, and it takes a long time to build a trusted relationship. You cannot take a purely economic principle which works in the matured procurement process of the western part of the world to the eastern side and then say, "I will just sell and then move on. Somebody else will manage the account." When you work in that geography, across all sizes of accounts they prefer the same person to be both hunter and farmer.

Clearly it is important to factor in the cultural expectations. If you don't, you can find your company making costly mistakes with important global customers. From Valerie's point of view, there are multiple considerations involved in the personnel allocation decision, with culture definitely among the most important:

> I've seen both models, and it's really important to determine the model that works for your business. You need to define attributes of your team, their skill sets and preferences. I don't like the total handoff; I prefer an advocacy role. You can end up not hunting or farming well enough, and not growing the account well enough. Those teams have to work together.

> I see companies that don't feel they are doing a good enough job on either side of that equation. If you do handoffs, if the whole team is engaged and the roles are explained to the client so they know ahead of time, you can probably do purposeful handoffs that are meaningful.

> How your company is organized affects how you serve your customer and how your customers buy. It goes back to your planned process and a good CRM. You need global oversight but local culture and relationships are important. Doing more business with your accounts is a big source of growth.

> —VALERIE BONEBRAKE

Valerie's perspective that some companies are dissatisfied with their performance with either hunters or farmers suggests that there is much more to learn in handling global account sales and account management. It's not only the structure and personnel roles that matter, although your own company's sales structure is an essential starting point.

Melissa explains a big problem for dedicated account managers, especially if they are also expected to develop all of the new opportunities within an account:

> As part of the "hunter" organization, you typically find highly skilled individuals, good closers focused on nothing more than closing a specific sales cycle. They know what they're doing, and can get in and get out of an opportunity relatively quickly.
>
> From a global account manager perspective, a sales executive that has an ongoing relationship with a specific account, they tend to become entrenched in all aspects of the account in an effort to build long lasting, strong relationships. The customer is not confused about where to go, and if done properly, the account manager can become a trusted advisor. In companies where you have numerous offerings and a finite set of accounts, repeat business is extremely important.
>
> The problem under this sales scenario is that everything funnels to the account manager; whether you've got a product issue, an implementation issue or an AR or invoicing issue, everything is escalated to the account manager. You can become so immersed in administrivia that there is little time for sales activities; it is often hard to find a good balance.
>
> —MELISSA DONNELLY

Hari defines an additional role, in which both farmers and hunters who do business inside a global account are managed by a person who orchestrates everything that happens with the named account:

The roles at any client include a hunter, which is the sales guys who sell various offerings; a farmer, a person who's doing service delivery and continues on the back of delivery to sell more, and the third is the game keeper who keeps the relationships in place in continuously morphing global organizations as well as makes sure that the hunters don't hunt the wrong way, or farmers don't farm the wrong thing. The game keeper will engage a variety of hunters and farmers and many other subject matter experts at a client, according to the client needs.

—HARI SHANKARANARAYANAN

Hari will engage a variety of hunters and farmers and many other subject matter experts in an account, according to the work he is orchestrating with the client and what they are trying to accomplish at a given time.

Melissa defines a similar role within her global account team:

In my group, since we are a strategic account organization, we have a role referred to as the Global Service Director. In most instances this group have very few accounts and concentrate specifically on ongoing projects. They help with project resourcing, escalations, governance processes, and other service related functions as well as carrying a services revenue objective.

—MELISSA DONNELLY

Subject Matter Experts

When you are working with global accounts, it's definitely not only the sales people who get involved in new deals. Today's buyers want to meet your subject matter experts (SMEs)—your technology team, customer service team, product team, engineers, R&D specialists, the people who design and install your products and services as well as the people who keep them going and working properly. Regardless of whether you use the terminology of hunters and farmers, many sales roles come into play. Sid identifies another role:

> *We have built a team called digital presales, which you can think of as "inside" presales. They work collaboratively with our inside sales teams and our partners to engage prospects throughout the buyer's journey. For example, if we're talking with a prospect that we believe has a high propensity to buy our solution, our digital presales team is available on demand to deliver a demo on the spot. They work hand-in-hand with inside sales and partners, both in identification of new opportunities and progressing existing opportunities to closure.*
>
> —SID KUMAR

Presales is a role at Rachel's company, including value engineers, who report to her. She explains how other subject matter experts and technical people get involved in the sale:

> *We try to use SMEs at varying points in the cycle. Value Engineering is a relatively new pre sales function that we use at the beginning of sales cycles to inspire the customer about the ROI that they can achieve. One important aspect of this team is that it helps us understand our prospects much more deeply because they use actual customer data to build a customized business case. It's a great opportunity to get close to the customer, to learn a lot about their business, build rapport, gain access and ultimately become a trusted advisor.*
>
> *What I initially saw with how the sales team tried to leverage Value Engineering was people not exactly knowing how to appropriately leverage the function. They would say," Maybe I need a value engineer on this." And they'd say, "Well, the*

meeting's tomorrow." As a Value Engineering team we always come back with, "No, you need to push that meeting," because it's so critical to prepare with the team and make sure everyone knows their role and what we're trying to accomplish.

It's the sales leader's responsibility to make sure that their team is spending enough time preparing and planning as a unit, what role each person's going to have, who each person needs to try to map to become trusted advisors with, what outcome they ideally need to get from their interactions, those kinds of things.

I think it's also important to bring a diverse group of people in all throughout the sale to appropriately map the account, because near the close of a negotiation invariably somebody's going to start to get a bit of cold feet. If you had a services person in early, for example, she has earned some trust and then when the time comes and I need to bring her in at the end to say, "Hey, it's going to be okay. We've done this a million times before and we'll make you successful" the prospect will always have a much higher confidence level. I think that's also really critical.

—RACHEL BARGER

Mircea currently manages a huge global region for a smaller company. He has a team that makes the sale. How do they then deliver it? Mircea defined a model in which project management becomes a fulcrum between sales and technical delivery and support. It allows a salesperson to hand off from the initial sale, but to be available to the project team, and most likely come back to lead the next sale as well:

It's important to have the same components of the team. The one who started as a Project Manager understands the client's need and has insight about the client.

He can follow up. When clients call, they can get directly to the PM, because it's annoying to have many explanations when you have an issue, or when you have something malfunction, things like that.

The same salesperson is still involved, but the project manager follows the project. It's not so much standardized in companies; not every company has a project manager doing the same thing. We see the project manager as the one who makes the alignment between sales and technical. The PM has to be sure that both the salesperson and the client are satisfied throughout our project, and with our product. The salesperson is the one to interact with the client, but also we get our technical people with their technical people so we don't lose meanings when we translate things from technical to sales to technical. They are different languages.

—MIRCEA SARACUT

This is a useful model for a small company building its presence around the world, without the resources to assign a full-time farmer to each account. It's not customary for the project manager to have a direct, ongoing relationship with sales. In fact, it's hard to make that happen, when you have employees working inside a global account but they are not sharing information about what's going on—they are only focused on delivering their project. Deliberately expanding that role will help.

Dedicated Accounts

In this chapter I've been primarily discussing accounts that have the potential to become large enough to warrant considerable resources from your sales and sales support people. Explicitly, here's what I mean. Once you have global customers to whom you sell a service that they will need over and over, or that they may want to expand to other locations or lines of business, then it makes sense to consider them "named accounts" with a dedicated individual or team to manage the relationship and guide the customers to making additional buying choices that will continue to prove valuable to them.

A team dedicated to a single account is essential if your competitors have a dedicated team, or if your company is innovating rapidly and has new versions or entirely new solutions to offer within a couple of years from your initial sale, or if you have a big solution that can move to other divisions or lines of business.

There are other customers that are unlikely to bring you additional very large new business that would have to be actively sold into new locations or new lines of business, but the same people that you sold in the first place might buy additional services. In that case, an inside sales team—a kind of farmer team—might manage those accounts instead of a dedicated team.

Introducing New Products and Services

Sometimes the account structure is overridden for special purposes or circumstances. I see this happening in many of the global companies themselves, when they create, for example, a Cloud team that provides specific services and product/solutions ideas to any of the named account sales teams.

This practice has the most success when the specialized sales team collaborates with the sellers that already have experience with the account, whether they are a dedicated team or not. It is always better to have a previously known person make the introduction to a new, specialized sales person or team. Without good coordination, the customer can easily believe that your company does not have its act together regarding them. Think of the customer first, and you will make the best decisions.

Lack of coordination when something changes, such as a new service line or new product, creates resentment and confusion among your sales team, which is bad for business in general. It is also unfair and discourteous to your customers. This kind of discontinuity sabotages your overall sales performance.

Resellers/Partners

A model that requires distinct roles when it comes to hunters and farmers is the reseller model. This is especially true in the IT industry where we typically find inside sales and field sales teams. Consider the distributors, who are the fulcrum between global IT manufacturers and networks of sales partners—smaller and larger resellers—serving businesses around the world. This complex and collaborative sales environment is what Kirk is responsible for at Ingram Micro:

The one constant in the IT industry is change. From technology solutions to service models, innovation and specialization are two areas where this industry thrives. Another area where the industry doesn't compromise is relationships.

We cross train our inside and field base teams – the hunters and farmers - to ensure they know the business, recognize the opportunity and are adding value across the entire IT lifecycle. Typically, these two teams collaborate under the guidance of a regional sales leader. If our efforts are global, we assign a global team leader to work across the regions with the executives to ensure collaboration and consistency.

We go deep with specializations, business and vertical expertise to help our channel partners grow more profitably and with precision. In the world of IT services, the talent (i.e. sales and support) is equally as important as the technology you provide. And the technology means nothing if the gains don't meet the business goals.

—KIRK ROBINSON

In a mature company, like Kirk's, many resources are devoted to the key customers as well as to other partners. The collaboration of hunters and farmers within key accounts greatly facilitates taking a customer's point of view. Of course, nothing involving people is ever a fixed system. When you are working with global accounts in which the parent company may have hundreds of subsidiaries, none of this is simple.

In Sid's company, inside sales teams are collocated throughout the world, as he describes:

> We have major hubs in each sales region around the world. There's real value to collocating our inside sales teams rather than having them dispersed. There's a lot of synergy and sharing of best practices when you are sitting right next to your colleagues in the same physical location. We've found that this strategy has been key to driving greater productivity.

—SID KUMAR

Although it would be nice to have clear demarcations of who does what in the sales organization, it never works that seamlessly. There are always classification questions as well as relationship questions. So smart sales organizations plan ahead, to ensure that their teams are accustomed to how an issue will be resolved when more than one sales person or team expects to get the same account.

If you want to hunt a global customer in multiple countries where it is doing business, you must figure out a team approach. It's not enough to have a large salesforce with territories all over the world. Your sales team needs to be exceptionally well-prepared to do their job with collaborative support. You will also have to incentivize people to work as a team and invest in and train special salespeople with significant experience in these global roles.

We have seen how some smaller companies grow into global businesses strategically, with a much smaller salesforce and a series of strategic decisions. Most often they learn to manage one global account, or they take on only one region and one line of business to start. Often they make strategic acquisitions of a well-run smaller company, whose personnel provide local knowledge and capabilities to their new partners. Once they get a solid start in a new region, they try to solidify where they are before they move out again to another new region.

Inside Sales

The Harvard Business Review reported in 2013 that "over the past two years, 46% percent of study participants reported a shift from a field sales model to an inside sales model, while 21% reported a shift from inside sales to a field sales model." [Steve W. Martin, *The Trend that is Changing Sales, November 4, 2013]* Another *HBR* article cited three key factors for shifting towards inside sales: cost-cutting pressure, technology advancements for ways to connect with customers, and buyers' acceptance and even preference for what I would call a virtual or remote connection rather than a direct connection to a salesperson. [*Andris A. Zoltners, PK Sinha, and Sally E. Lorimer, The Growing Power of Inside Sales*, July 29, 2013]

> *I look at inside sales as the team of individuals within the organization that is finding new opportunities, building pipeline, and helping convert that pipeline into book business.*
>
> *It's simple as looking at where there's opportunity, building that pipeline. In all cases they're doing that. In some cases, they're working with the field and with partners to close the transaction, and in other cases they're doing it end to end either directly on our paper or with a partner.*
>
> *The one variable would be how far along the cycle does the team take it. Do they take it all the way to the end, or do*

they work with the field to transact that to the end, or with a partner to transact that to the end? The reality is I look at inside sales as just working on the exact same thing a field sales rep would work on, except you're focused on a volume and velocity type of play and penetrating new accounts.

—SID KUMAR

How much the shift to inside sales affects working with global customers remains to be seen. There is clearly still a preference for field salespeople to work on large accounts, face to face with customers, especially multinational and global accounts.

There is also the systems integrator, a person or company that may be helping your clients integrate software components from multiple suppliers. Even if you are not selling software systems, your clients may be engaging other consultants to help them make a wide range of enterprise decisions, and you may encounter them frequently. Getting to know these consultants, educating them about your products and capabilities, and helping them to help your customers are smart strategies.

Intermediaries

Sometimes the global company itself is not really your customer, or at least is not a customer to whom you can sell directly. With the increasing use of Business Process Outsourcing services, Procurement Outsourcing (PO) is predicted to grow by another 12% over the next five years. [HfS 2013 Procurement Outsourcing Blueprint] When a company outsources its buying services, which many large companies do, you as a seller may be kept at arm's length or longer from the end users of your services. In a sense, the procurement operation becomes your buyer, and its representatives the people with whom you need to build strong relationships. Clearly it's important to understand how your prospective customer buys as you identify the people that you need to meet.

Increasingly, I find an intermediary company between you and the end user. It's always been common on a big construction project to have a general contractor who wins the overall contract but hires multiple subcontractors during the course of the project. If you are often in the subcontractor role, if that's where you want to be, or if you are losing out to bigger competitors, it may be fruitful for you to cultivate one or more large general contractors who would hire you routinely on projects that are otherwise out of your reach.

But in a newer version of the general contractor, individuals and firms act as consultants, or customer's agents, responsible for managing the procurement process for a single project or many similar projects. They may be in an advisory role to the end user or they may be even closer to the actual buying decision.

People in other roles may be involved in advising your current and potential customers when it comes to certain kinds of technology sales. I asked Melissa if her teams actively cultivate those solutions and systems integrators who are advising her global clients:

> We work closely with a number of System Integrators. Often they'll make introductions for us and work closely with us to bring an opportunity to fruition. Many of our key SI partners have in-depth knowledge of our solutions. We often train and educate existing SI partners on new solutions to broaden their skills and overall offering to our joint customers.
>
> If you have a strong network of systems integrators in the field that know, understand and are selling your solutions, it will most certainly increase your opportunity for success.

—MELISSA DONNELLY

How you allocate your people to open global accounts and to continue selling new business to these accounts is critically important.

Everyone agrees that companies leave money on the table all the time with global accounts. As you can see, you need to solve a whole range of challenging problems in order to work with them successfully to their satisfaction as well as yours.

I've seen estimates of how much more energy it takes to sell a new product to a new customer than to sell an existing product to an existing customer. I suspect that these little formulae come from sales of topcoats or appliances or hand tools or books rather than enterprise software or logistics or engineering solutions. Nevertheless, it makes sense that you should nurture your global accounts to the very best of your ability in a spirit of innovation derived from deep knowledge and carefully allocated teams.

WHALE HUNTING TIPS ON PEOPLE

Roles. The responsibilities of "hunters" and "farmers" have changed and continue to change as the needs of global customers change. Be sure you consider new role definitions as you introduce changes. Don't let whale hunting become a prize—with smaller accounts being perceived as only for losers. Likewise, don't let whale hunting become a popularity contest or a reward for length of service!

Options. The way you allocate your sales and account management personnel has many variations, involving everything from the size of your company to the nature of your business to your introduction of new products and services. The Whale Hunting way is to make those decisions deliberately and not be afraid to change when change seems necessary.

Culture. With global clients, you need to understand their global corporate culture but also the local culture of each location. To best serve your customers, invest in local resources with local knowledge.

Territories. Don't allow your company's practices or policies to become overly territorial. Sales managers need to override territories if you discover that another salesperson has longer or better relationships with the customer. It's all about the customers, not you.

Opportunities. Most companies do not do the best job they could of acquiring new business with their current large accounts. Your global sales teams have great potential to influence your top line and bottom line when they are strategically deployed.

CHAPTER 6

INTEGRATE MARKETING

First you have to have the right people on the team. I've seen many a CMO that is afraid of revenue responsibility, that doesn't see that as marketing's job. I literally talked to a VP of marketing and explained the work that we do. I describe us as sales pipeline people, we do demand generation, we do sales pipeline development work. You understand, we're basically marketers.

But after I described what we do, she said, "Oh that sounds great, but I'd have to hook you up with my VP of sales. I'd be mostly interested in help with marketing." Literally she told me that; it almost knocked me out of my chair. I can't believe ...! On her bio it said something about strategic development of marketing collateral as part of her responsibilities.

I think of that and I think there are still plenty of people in marketing that just aren't going to be able to make this leap right now. Hopefully they will later, or they're probably just not going to find a job. You have to have the right people in the right seats.

—MATT HEINZ

Hostility between sales and marketing is one of the most common circumstances that I encounter when I'm working with a new client.

It's also probably the most damaging and costly.

Marketing generates leads. Implements a new, more robust CRM to track all the leads. Trains the sales reps on the new CRM. Laments to management that sales won't cooperate. Sales is busy with existing leads and projects. Doesn't see the value in the CRM and can't be bothered with filling in more details online. Still has to produce a weekly spreadsheet for their boss. Always putting out fires.

At best, the two groups are polite but distant. At worst, they are in open warfare.

One of the quickest ways to recognize that problem, however, is to go after global clients. Suddenly the stakes are much higher, the ground to cover much wider, and the mutual needs much deeper. Here's what Matt has to say:

> My background is primarily on the marketing side, but I'll be the first to tell you that I think one reason that sales and marketing have not been able to align well in the past is really marketing's fault. I say that somewhat facetiously, but I think marketing has been slow to accept revenue responsibility, marketing has been slow to understand and embrace the fact they need to be measured based on revenue output of their work. They need to be measured based not on leads, not on awareness, not on the means but on the ends. I think up front **fundamentally marketing needs to accept revenue responsibility**; they need to know that they're going to be measured on revenue contribution, on sales pipeline contribution.
>
> The minute marketing starts thinking about themselves as a profit center and not a cost center it's starting to move in the right direction. There are two fundamental building blocks beyond a mindset of understanding and embracing revenue

responsibility. One is common objectives and two is common definitions of what are we working towards. I see all the time marketing organizations will have a marketing-qualified lead goal. Most of the time that goal has nothing to do with the sales number; no single model has been developed that says "to hit this sales number we need to get this big a pipeline."

To get that pipeline we need this many leads, here's what percent of those leads are going to come from marketing; therefore, that's what we need from marketing. It's a fairly simple model to build and yet few companies do that so that both teams come to the table and know exactly what is needed quantifiably to hit the number.

You better have consistent definitions. You could have a global demand center that's got one definition and field marketing that has another, yet with that inconsistency it will be impossible to model and to forecast what you're going to achieve.

—MATT HEINZ

Customer expectations are at the heart of this need to integrate sales and marketing functions. Today, two key adaptations attempt to meet this need: content marketing and sales enablement. Customers continually educate themselves on what's available in the market-place, so you must become prominent as a company that provides this kind of information—which is quite different from product-fo-cused marketing materials. You also need to continually equip your global sales team with customer-specific materials and tools, with just-in-time marketing services.

Sales needs marketing to contribute throughout the sales process, not just in lead generation. As we have seen, many salespeople working global accounts spend all of their time with named accounts, so the traditional type of lead generation is of no consequence to them. Rather, they need to know more about the company and its people, changes in structure and people's positions, industry knowledge and news, and the kind of outcomes that they could achieve that would move them forward in concert with their strategic objectives.

As Sid explains, from his perspective heading up global inside sales:

> It's about generating new opportunities, building high quality pipeline and converting this pipeline into revenue. We need to be 100% aligned and in lockstep with marketing throughout the sales cycle in order to be successful. If we're not aligned, we may find ourselves rowing in opposite directions and not getting anywhere.
>
> —SID KUMAR

One sales individual, or a small team, may be completely responsible for a small number of global accounts—maybe only one account, or only two or three depending upon the size of the account and the extent of your business and your opportunity with the account. For that team to function at its highest level, marketing fulfills critical roles. Customer demands and expectations drive marketing and sales closer than ever:

> One of the fundamental changes in the B2B sales process is the role played by our marketing team across each stage of the buying cycle – awareness, research and ongoing education. We are continuing to work closer with our marketing and business development teams to provide a much more personalized marketing experience. We maintain a regular cadence with both the marketing and business development teams. They are included in team meetings, business reviews and weekly calls so that they have a good

understanding of our accounts, the opportunities we are working, our account white space as well as accounts and opportunities which we are struggling to develop.

—MELISSA DONNELLY

A strategic account marketing team is dedicated to large global accounts, just as is a dedicated sales team. These teams must work seamlessly. If you have only recently begun to assign specific salespeople to focus on specific industries, or whenever you are approaching a new industry, there is an important strategic role for the marketing team, as Valerie observes:

It's a best practice to engage marketing early—they can play a huge part in learning the industry and also how to penetrate that industry.

—VALERIE BONEBRAKE

Customers are nervous about awarding a contract to a company that has no particular experience in their industry, regardless of how similar your service might play out in any number of industries. Of course, it's extremely frustrating as you grow to get into each new industry because you need a customer first in order to get that experience!

Marketing can help the sales team understand an industry and how to break in to it, and they can provide sales assistance as your team is learning more about particular companies and their key people. As Matt explained:

There's a significant level of intelligence and message development that marketing can enable for sales as well. For instance, your ability to follow people on a social channel, set up listening tools, so the reps are able to listen and engage with prospects. To develop daily, weekly listening platforms to understand what's going on in an organization and get early signals of when things have changed or when new situations have occurred that create urgency for your product or service.

—MATT HEINZ

In the last chapter we looked at how important it is to align inside sales with field sales in order to gain real traction with global accounts. But marketing must be part of the alignment as well. Sometimes we continue to do things because that's how we've done them, but we discover it no longer works that way. Where marketing and sales most often disagree is on lead generation. But with global accounts, it's not that you need a high quantity of leads. You've moved far beyond leads—you need a continuous flow of information between sales and marketing about the customer, the market, the people, new opportunities, ideas from other industries—everything specialized and customized for your global customer.

I asked Matt if he thinks marketing and sales will eventually become a fully-integrated function. Here's what he said:

In many companies they are, the answer is absolutely. We've got a couple clients today, where there is one individual who manages both sales and marketing. They're forcing that to happen, but I think by example they're demonstrating how it can happen. By example, they're showing that the entire organization is focused on hitting a number. It doesn't mean that they aren't prioritizing marketing efforts that don't drive an immediate response. And it doesn't mean that they've given up on brand or given up on PR or given up on content. It means there is a singular focus on the outputs that matter. I don't think it requires having one person on both functions but I do think the alignment of objectives and alignment around incentives is key to accelerating that cooperation in more companies.

—MATT HEINZ

You "name" an account—identify it by name as being of special importance to you—because of its potential to continuously provide you with new opportunities. But your customers expect more of you than you may be considering. The customer wants to feel special. They want something addressed especially to them. They want you to sell to them—not their segment—just to them. "One size fits all" is no longer viable. What this means in practice is that the longer you work with a global customer, the more they will expect you to consult with them on potential solutions to their current business problems and opportunities. Not only about your product or service—about their business. Sales cannot do this without a strong marketing team engaged with them.

Mircea is now starting up new sales teams in countries throughout Europe and Asia. The need to have sales and marketing on the same team is acute for his company:

> Even my quest just changed in six months, because I have to address new markets in different countries. I have to have a new sales team each time. The biggest asset is having a small team in sales and marketing. Things are working smoother, because if you don't have well-communicating sales and marketing departments, if your sales is not aligned with your marketing, then you can be way off track. When you are discussing sales over several countries, it can be quite a mess. You have to attune each message for each target audience, being sure to have an ear on sales as a marketing department, because it's like throwing the rock in a pit. You count the seconds before you get the reaction!

> To know your market, you have always to listen to the market through your sales guy's feedback. The salespeople need to bring the feedback to marketing and to work together in creating for each niche, for each new market, a new mix that in time will prove successful. It's not always an instant hit; not

each prospect is a good fit. You try to make the most of each interaction to show that, on one hand you're a professional. On the other hand, you are, especially, a human being who understands the customer's needs, to show that it's more important to help them and make them your longtime partner, or, at least friend, than to have a quick grab of a check.

—MIRCEA SARACUT

Mircea talks about how important it is for marketing to learn from sales about what's going on in the field. How about the role of marketing in providing sales the information they need about a prospective customer? Matt has a key perspective on that:

You've got a lot of people in the industry talking about account based marketing as a new area. I think there's been a lot of value in the tools and the focus on account based marketing. Of course, sales people are shaking their heads saying, "Account based sales, we've been doing that forever, thank you marketing for coming to the table." Still, it's exciting to see marketing saying, "We can market like that; we can be more precise." It's almost the anti-inbound. Inbound marketing is all about just throwing something out there and seeing who responds. Account based marketing says, "We only care about these people. Let's focus our efforts on them."

—MATT HEINZ

Forbes Insights backs up Matt's claim: "Three-fourths of top-performing organizations have strong alignment between sales and marketing; poorly performing companies notably do not." [*Forbes Insights* with Brainshark. "The Power of Enablement." 2015.]

Matt's comments are also aligned with Whale Hunting. When you are hunting whales, you always have specific targets, prospective companies that you know are ideal for you. The rest of the market is immaterial to the whale hunting team. Not to say that smaller customers aren't important, but you approach them differently and with different people.

Clearly, sales and marketing functions need to be deeply integrated. Today that is not as common a model as it should be and inevitably will become not too far into the future. The competitive advantage goes to those companies who do the best job of integrating their cross-functional teams in specific service to their global customers.

For that reason, I recommend a dedicated marketing team for global accounts, a team with shared responsibility for P&L on the accounts. Every sales and global account management team needs access to a marketing team with responsibility for the account. If an account manager is required to carry three global accounts, a global account marketing team should be aligned with the same three accounts. Maybe that is one marketing person who is responsible for directing some of marketing's efforts towards global accounts. Or depending on your company size, maybe that's a multi-person team dedicated to working with sales on new sales and repeat with global accounts.

Consider the money you leave on the table today because of shortcomings in your key account services. Investing in a strategic marketing team for global accounts makes that team part of a profit center instead of an expense.

WHALE HUNTING TIPS ON MARKETING

Coopetition. The sales and marketing relationship should be one in which the teams are incentivized to work closely together, in cooperation, as well as to challenge the other to win, in competition.

Trend. There is a very clear trend bringing marketing and sales together into a functional area, often called sales enablement. Encourage this trend in your company.

Advantage. Companies who manage to closely align sales and marketing will see a huge competitive advantage in their large account sales process. From how money is spent on these functions to what messages your sales team delivers to clients, a collaborative approach will serve to differentiate you from competitors.

Singularity. Each global customer is a market of one. Only with sales and marketing working closely together can you convey this awareness to your customer, producing new evidence on a regular basis that you are directly focused on them.

Roles. The roles of both marketing and sales have changed significantly as more companies have been managing global accounts in the internet age. Help your teams understand how to adopt new roles that are suitable for a new world.

STRUCTURE SUMMARY

The lessons from Part 2 reflect important strategic decisions about your sales infrastructure: how you organize your company's sales functions and how you deploy your people. Clarity of roles is a core principle of Whale Hunting, but it's important not to let internal roles get so rigid that they compromise your company's ability to do your best work. Whale Hunters say, "Focus on the hunt, not the hunter." That's just a reminder that large account sales require a highly collaborative approach involving many different people and roles within your company as well as within your customers' companies.

PART III

PROCESS: BEYOND STEPS

WHALE HUNTING PERSPECTIVES

Whale Hunters use the term "shaman" to denote a sales leader with sales representatives reporting to him or her, at all levels from a territory sales manager to an Executive VP of Global Sales. The Inuit shaman, or holy person, was a spiritual guide and healer, having the ability to visit the spirit world as well as the temporal world. The shaman was a teacher and mentor, transmitting the historical wisdom of the tribe to new generations. Together, the shaman and harpooner (the salesperson) are responsible for leading a safe and successful hunt. The more complex the hunt, as in global account sales, the more important it is for the shaman and harpooner to plan for the hunt and to prepare for the hunt they will undertake each year.

This chapter is primarily about the roles of the sales leaders who have responsibility for global sales teams. It's about managing global sales teams, seeing to their training and professional development, coaching them, and overseeing your company's formal sales process for global accounts. It's all about facilitating the operation of a sales organization throughout a long and complex sale by means of a deliberate, replicable yet flexible sales processes.

CHAPTER 7

THE SELLERS' PROCESS

It's a far too familiar case. You've had your eye on a global whale for quite some time, but you don't really know them at all. You've heard that they are planning a big expansion—a major new facility in a new region—and you know there will be some big roles for a company like yours. You manage to meet with a couple of engineers who tell you that an RFP will be issued, but it will not be released for about 18 months.

The engineers refer you to a procurement specialist, who agrees to put your name on the list of companies to receive the Request for Proposals.

You're pretty excited! When you get back to the office, you happily add this company to your personal prospect list in the CRM, move the prospect to the "opportunity" stage, and add your new buyer friend to the contact list. Maybe you even mark a follow-up date for a year or so from now.

Sure enough, two full years later your company finally receives a massive RFP from the target company. The first time they've ever included you on their list! You put some people together to work on the proposal—and it's a big one, by gosh. Through frenetic work by sales, operations, legal, finance and marketing, you manage to get this proposal out the door in the nick of time! You move this deal from "opportunity" to "proposal" stage (the CRM marks it 60% probable to win now!!) and you wait.

What are your real odds of winning?

Of course you didn't win that bid. You didn't even come close. Because while your team was off doing other things until the RFP came out, one or more of your competitors was spending lots of time with that company, meeting with everyone who would talk to her, hosting a special meeting with members of her executive team at the trade show, and in general learning everything there was to know about the target company, their plans for expansion, and their decision-making process. Your team could have done all those things, but didn't. In fact, they just didn't know to do anything different.

One of the most important jobs for a sales leader is to help the company define its sales process and to redefine that process whenever circumstances change. More often than not, however, the sales process is created by default or with minimal customization from whatever Customer Relationship Management (CRM) system is being used. Often it is Marketing that selects the CRM; or there is an enterprise system or vendor preference that dictates the choice of a CRM. Even when Sales makes the call, the portion of the CRM that manages the sales process may not receive much customization.

Sales process is a huge problem when it comes to global sales, especially as we continue to implement automated CRM systems. A "sales process" is typically represented by a linear sequence of steps and is often a "one size fits all" practice. Although CRMs promise fluidity and flexibility, and many deliver on that promise to some extent as far as managing data, you will still be dealing with a representation that begins as a straight line from here to there.

114

For example, these steps constitute one company's sales process as defined by their CRM:

- Lead
- Inquiry
- Presentation
- Proposal
- Follow Up/Negotiation
- Commitment to Buy
- PO/Purchase Order

In this example, each step is a noun—a lead, a presentation, a proposal, and so on. The sales team is invited to think of either the beginning state or the end state of that step, and no real interaction is connoted except in follow up/negotiation.

Another sales process looks like this:

- Qualification
- Needs Analysis
- Proposal Delivered
- Verbal Agreement
- Closed/Won
- Closed/Lost

In this second case, the name for each step implies more activity —"qualification" has the connotation of a process in comparison to "lead" or "inquiry." Still, the team that uses this system has no steps defined between, say, "needs analysis" and "proposal!"

These are typical, even standard, processes—defined by steps that came with the CRM out of the box or even customized for their company's use. It doesn't matter. What matters is that a process that looks like these won't help your sales team conduct a sale to a global company.

To take the first list as an example, you might work with a global company for months to go from your "Qualification" to their agreement to let you conduct a "Needs Analysis." And what work would it take to go from "Needs Analysis" to "Proposal?" Or in the second instance, to go from "Presentation" to "Proposal?"—unless that "Presentation" had followed goodness knows how many meetings and other interactions prior to a "Proposal."

It just doesn't work like this. So a sales team who is supposed to be following a list of process steps is being cheated out of all kinds of help, ideas, and information about all of the activities that have to happen between the steps.

And having sat in on many, many weekly sales meetings, I promise you that unless the sales rep is actively working on the "presentation" or an actual "proposal," each weekly sales report is like the one before—"we're working on it."

In a complex sale, most of the difficult sales work takes place in between the documented steps. There is simply not a good way within a typical CRM system to record or explain the steps. How do you explain in a process map or a CRM that at this step "you may need to talk with twenty people, representing seven departments, and you will need to use your sales support specialists to come along with you and meet their counterparts, Oh, and this is how you should prepare them to be part of your sales process?" It's just not possible. That doesn't mean ditch the sales process or ditch the CRM! They both have a critically important role in managing a large sale.

But you need exceptional tools to help your sales teams manage a large account, especially a global account. The sheer amount of data you will acquire and create with a global account is difficult to represent and share. The typical CRM, even a dynamic and highly customized one, may not be sufficient for the complex account planning that a huge account requires.

A key element of The Whale Hunting Process™ is to work from the Whale Hunting model to map a specific large-account sales process for your own company. ProPharma Group is my Whale Hunting client representative in this book, so I asked Jeff what is working and what is not working so far in his company's implementation of that process. At the time of this writing, they had been at it for about eighteen months, which Jeff relates is a typical length of time for them to be nearing the end but not yet completed on big deals.

> It seems to be working okay so far. I say that in that we're still in the hunt on many of the large opportunities. The largest opportunities that we just started as we were learning and coming through the whole whale hunting process are just now coming to fruition. In fact, we have a team of people that's down at a finalist presentation today on one of those. That I think will give us some good data as to how these things are going. We think it's helping us. It certainly has helped refine our process, helped refine our decision-making, helped us to be more disciplined in our decision-making, particularly by empowering us to make "go and no-go" decisions. We didn't make many no-go decisions before this, and so it's really brought that to the forefront of our conversations.

> One thing I saw just a few days ago that made me just smile. In the slightly more remote part of our company, medical information, they've resisted a lot of the traditional sales processes, and now we are proposing on an extremely large opportunity that would really double that side of the business. I went in to review that proposal through our CRM system the other day, and when I went in to where all the

documents were stored, there was the RFP story, there was the Buyers' Table. Many of the whale hunting documents were sitting right there, and nobody beat those guys with a stick to use those tools! That's the team telling me from the ground floor that these are things of value, and we use them to help us figure out how to win this project. I thought that was probably the best piece of evidence.

—JEFF HARGROVES

As Jeff describes, a Whale Hunting sales process includes instructions to complete each of the planning tools that help at each step; tools are linked to process steps. What they call a "step" may encompass a good deal of time and the use of multiple planning tools. ProPharma Group has built their process into their CRM and also into specific Standard Operating Procedures (SOPs) to which all sales employees are trained and which they use as they are selling.

The problem for them, as with almost of all of my clients, is that many of the "steps" in a sales process are actually "stages"—a considerable period of time during which a wide range of activities needs to take place, and which activities those are depends on variable circumstances. So when they get involved in a global whale hunt, they come to periods of time when they are repeating steps, or extending steps beyond when they could seriously be called a "step!"

In some cases, a standard sales process would make sales activity easier, more efficient, and more successful. But not necessarily for a large, complex global account. Other systems have terms like "Qualify—site visit—proposal—negotiation" and so on, equally hampered by big gaps in the process.

When I asked Lisa if her clients follow a sales process rigorously, she laughed:

Follow a sales process rigorously? This is one of the first questions I ask my clients! The answers vary. Most small companies do not have a sales process of their own. Midsize companies have a growing recognition that they need a process, especially if they are going to invest in a CRM like Salesforce. The CRM will either follow their sales process or become their new sales process (not an ideal scenario). Big companies generally have a sales process, with mobile access—but in my experience, few sales people, despite their manager's insistence and the benefits that can be gained, actually follow it rigorously. However, I do see adherence when a thoughtful and comprehensive change management plan is executed before, during and after roll out of the process.

—LISA MAGNUSON

An enterprise sale creates a major change in how parts of that company do business. Think of the change involved in adopting a new CRM, changing logistics providers, outsourcing spend management, or implementing a new sales process. Chances are your supplier or vendor has not married their implementation process to a change management process.

Your global customers fear change; they hate it. It's hard, it's painful, and most of the time the outcomes to them are not worth the effort. Change means more work, more complaints, more fuss. So you will encounter this during the sales process as well as implementation. Define a good change management plan to coincide with implementation of your new tools, and make it a plan that your team will manage for the customer. This will give you a clear edge over your competitors.

Valerie points out that the sales process for big account deals needs to be sufficiently robust to accommodate the complicated nature of that kind of deal. For her, it's more about assigning roles and responsibilities than it is about defining steps:

It gets a lot more complex. We had a formal sales process. My advice is first, do your homework on the industry and then have a really well thought-out sales process that gives clarity to all roles, with a repository of information that enables planning and captures the historical perspective. You're not selling to one person, and it's not one person selling. The basic first step of your sales process needs to be the Go/No Go decision—a set of questions to enable leadership to decide if this deal is worth pursuing. You also need a good review process before a proposal is submitted to the client.

Some opportunities are not worth pursuing, especially if the timeframe to respond is unrealistic and the customer is not willing to compromise. We would decline to bid if we couldn't do a good job in the time allotted. When the allowable time is just too short, then you are just a check bid, not a real contender.

We used the sales process to track opportunities and give visibility to steps. With a dispersed team, we had regular conference calls and we spent a lot of time educating on the competitive environment. Marketing was a big part of that.

—VALERIE BONEBRAKE

Valerie makes an important point about "a repository of information that enables planning." When you are working with a global account, you expect to have a whole series of opportunities—even some concurrent ones—while the typical CRM is more suitable to managing a particular opportunity.

That's why you need to move from *sales process* to *account planning*.

Account Planning

The account plan encompasses multiple opportunities within your global account. An account plan is a roadmap that helps you move from what you know to what you intend to do next. Most large-account salespeople have had some kind of sales training that includes how to create and use an account plan. In its simplest form, the account plan is a template to help a salesperson create a series of goals, objectives, and actions to manage a big opportunity. Sometimes the account plan is built into the CRM or attached to the CRM in some way to facilitate sharing. Nevertheless, it's a static document.

A more dynamic account plan is an online space to manage and share documents, such as *SharePoint (sharepoint.com)*. Some large-account teams combine document sharing with online conversation tools, like *Yammer (yammer.com)*, which integrates with SharePoint and other tools. Those platforms facilitate a more robust account planning methodology where information is easily shared such that it becomes "account knowledge" and not just personal knowledge.

The most elaborate account planning software platforms are action-oriented, "intelligent" systems. Integrated with your CRM, they provide various types of maps and other planning tools, typically with a coding system that helps a team to annotate contacts and opportunities as the account grows. What differentiates these tools is their ability to focus your attention on what needs to happen next based on what you already know or don't know. They don't just document your progress; they guide your team through an account management process that doesn't end when one opportunity is complete. One that has gained a lot of traction is *Dealmaker (the-tasgroup.com/dealmaker)*, integrated with salesforce.com.

Another very powerful Account Management platform is *Revegy (Revegy.com)*. I have worked with several dispersed teams that were implementing Revegy as an account management tool, integrated with salesforce.com. Melissa's company went through that process. Here's how she describes that adoption process:

> The adoption rate is slow due to the time required to input each of the initial data elements into the system. When you have an organization that is already very time starved, anything that eats into sales and customer activity is going to be a challenge. Though the initial steps are time consuming, I like the Revegy tool. It would be ideal if there was a mechanism to automate some of the initial required set up. As an example, we import contacts from Salesforce into the tool but often those contacts are out of date or have changed. As a result, the onus is on the sales people to keep everything updated and in sync. If there was a way to more closely synchronize the tools as well as maintain current information, it would be fantastic.

> If people take the time to use the tool, not just populate the tool but really use it as part of their overall ongoing strategic discussions, there is a tremendous amount of value. When you start really accessing and understanding the data, it becomes an invaluable tool. Helping to identify and understand your customer's business strategy or realizing aspects of their business in which you don't currently participate is where you begin to see immediate value.

> Additionally, you've got one place, one repository for all relevant data involving your accounts. You begin to develop a 360-degree view of that customer or that account. There is also turnover in any sales organization, thus the tool provides one consistent place to input and update all aspects of a customer or an opportunity so that new sales people can onboard much more quickly with consistent and accurate data.

> —MELISSA DONNELLY

No question there is a great deal of work to get a team up to speed on the Revegy tool. In my experience, training on the tool, coaching on how to implement the tool with a global account team, and ongoing reinforcement from sales management are all required. Like many of today's best tools, it strikes many salespeople as just one more demand on their time. The activity of populating various components of the program is indeed time-consuming, especially as a team process.

Nevertheless, as Melissa points out, once a team gets to the point of using the robust account planning tools—such as a draft strategic account plan to share and discuss with the customer—they will find it to be a real advantage in selling more business into their existing account.

The challenge is to select tools that are suited to enabling the sales team to work smarter, more collaboratively, and with less extra motion. The tool needs to offer the salesperson a huge return on investment for her efforts to learn it and to keep it up to date. More and more, the tools will be keeping themselves updated in service to the salespeople.

In support of account planning, beyond deal-planning, Sid addresses that period of time between the current deal and the next deal—what he calls "the post-sale plan." These are all the things that your team should be addressing with your customers who already have some of your products or services inside.

> It's important to consider the entire customer lifecycle, not just what it takes to get the current deal on the table done. What is your plan to make sure your customer gets a timely return on their investment and is successful for the long-run? Successful organizations place a great deal of emphasis on ensuring that their customers have an exceptional overall experience. This means that the post-sales plan is just as

important as the sales plan to win the deal. Are you making sure that their implementation goes smoothly? Are you making sure that your customer is aware of the product updates that are available to them? Do you have a plan to drive greater user adoption within the account? These are the types of questions to ask to ensure that you have happy and satisfied customers that could potentially be references and hopefully increase their share of wallet with you over time.

—SID KUMAR

The hunter who opened the first door may not have responsibility for any of these concerns. Perhaps it is your internal project manager. More likely it is an Account Manager—a farmer—who is at the same time responsible for identifying new opportunities inside the account.

How your team handles the post-sales journey has everything to do with your opportunities for continued additional business from a global account. The Whale Hunters' Process™ model is a continuous loop from an initial sale to repeat sales. After the "Hunt" phase comes the "Harvest," that phase during which your team delivers all that you have promised, and more, as well as undertaking all of the activities that will lead you strategically to the next opportunity.

A Long Sales Cycle

Hari walked me through a detailed explanation of how he used to manage a long sales cycle. I am including much of it here because it summarizes a real-world process as a set of three phases and helps to explain the kind of knowledge that each phase requires:

The long sales cycle happens in 3 different phases. The first phase is opening the door itself. You write 20 letters to 20 different people in an organization, you'd probably get meetings with 3 or 4 at best. To get the meetings is one phase which is long. Once you get the meeting, to convince them there's an opportunity is the second phase. But that is usually a series of presentations that one would go through, you would keep coming back and saying, "Give me some data, I will make a business case for you," or alternatively, say "A company of your size in a similar industry has done x, y, z, and got benefits, etc." Keep coming back with information; keep coming back with presentations to the same set of people over and over again.

—HARI SHANKARANARAYANAN

So Hari didn't have a "step" which says "get a first meeting" or "make a presentation." He explains his process in three phases, and in this first phase he would get meetings with multiple people, and he would meet with many people in the company, and he would come back to them repeatedly with new information and new ideas. So if you were teaching this process, you would represent it as a phase during which your job is to keep in touch with all of the key buyers, bringing them new information, new ideas, and new presentations.

Is there a typical time frame for the first stage? Hari doesn't define it like that. But I like to put some kind of time boundaries on the phases, or stages, so that my team can decide if anything is going wrong or if we are wasting time on a deal to which we should say NO!

The next phase in Hari's process involves a proposal:

After the opportunities crystallize, you get to a proposal stage. That's when the client's buying behavior comes into play, and it's a long stage because it's in the client's hands. Once you put in a proposal, look for a friend or an advisor in the client's buying table, someone who's willing to talk to you on a regular basis to coach your team, "This is where the deal is now, and it's going to take this much time. You need to talk to Mr X" etc. Also if you know the eventual buyer, the approver, and the negotiator, you should keep sending them information, even after the proposal, saying for example, "Did you know that since we sent you the proposal we signed another deal with one of the companies like you, in France? Here's some information on that." Or, "Did you know that one of our other clients had a successful result recently; would you like to talk to them? Here's the person you can talk to." Keep sending out such information. Even if it was in the periphery, you would always be there on their radar, somewhere on their radar.

—HARI SHANKARANARAYANAN

This behavior is critically important. As I said earlier, most defined sales processes don't include the most important steps: delivering the proposal is only a prelude to consistent regular communication after you complete a proposal. But of course, the sellers need to know what kind of regular communication might be useful, and they need to know what the customer expects.

In Hari's business, the process of contract negotiation typically goes according to plan once the customer makes a buying decision. For other global sellers, however, the third phase of a process—the negotiation phase—could be extremely complicated and fraught with the danger of not closing.

You simply must focus on customer expectations and customer needs, especially the need to override your CRM process if it's based on steps. The customer's process is not linear—you may need to repeat the same set of steps or mini-processes with multiple groups of people, or to introduce new steps or new ideas into the process at any time. It's not linear.

And the speed is so fast that the whole environment can change on a dime. That change doesn't mean you must lose or that you must start over. You must be prepared for the speed of change. And the fluidity of their process, and therefore your own.

A complex sale to a global customer really is far removed from a process; it's more accurately defined as a journey. And it's the buyers' journey, not the sellers.' Although as the next chapter discusses, it's the seller's responsibility to identify the right buyers and to lead them on their journey.

WHALE HUNTING TIPS FOR THE SELLERS' PROCESS

Customization. A standard sales process made up of steps, dictated by your CRM or copied from somewhere else, will be insufficient for the successful pursuit and management of a global account. Spend time with your sales and marketing team to craft a workable, fluid sales process focused on all the activities that may need to happen at various stages.

Selection. Be sure you define a clear Go/No Go decision point for any specific opportunity or deal. Specify the criteria that must be in place in order to reach that decision. Learn to recognize the best, most likely opportunities with the highest success rate and lowest cost of sale, and say NO to the rest.

Account Planning. A global account requires a strategic approach based on deep knowledge and understanding developed with the client's team and your own. If you put off all your strategic account planning to put out fires or deal only with the day to day, you are likely to fail. Keep time on your calendar for thinking and planning.

Tools. Provide your global sales team with technology tools to make their jobs easier, to encourage them to plan ahead, and to support them in acquiring deep knowledge about customers, industries, and markets. The best sales tools are not for managing metrics and reporting—that should be automated—but for their positive influence on best practices in your sales process.

Gaps. Even the best sales processes for large accounts will have huge gaps between typical steps—"qualifying" and "proposing," for example. And you may not have a step that says "create the vision" or "teach your customer what to do next." Go with stages, not steps, and provide exceptional training and coaching for your team to fill in the gaps.

CHAPTER 8

THE BUYERS' PROCESS

I love photography and I also love video. I like both media, and with photography it's sort of creating that moment, capturing that moment in time.

I was looking at a sequence of shots I took of a swan taking off when I was in a kayak, and I positioned myself so I had the right light ... and then I analyzed the photos and realized that swans actually don't take off out of water. They actually use their feet to run on water while they're flapping their wings!

Their feet, their webbing, sort of creates spray behind them, so it's really a wild sort of take off. They have to struggle with the water and pushing it away and bouncing off while they're lifting off.

To me photography is another way of seeing the world, of focusing on some details that we, by not looking through the lens, we wouldn't notice.

—GERHARD GSCHWANDTNER

I have mental images of swans, and in all my images they are exceedingly graceful, serene, quiet creatures. Never ungainly. So Gerhard's story surprised me, that the swans actually have to run on the water and create a churn in order to lift off!

I have images of global sales, too, and in my images they are equally graceful and serene. The ultimate outcomes are called into being through a beautiful dance between sellers and buyers.

These images, focused through the lens that reveals details we wouldn't otherwise see, surprise me too—because the outcomes are usually beautiful, but the process to get there is fraught with chaos.

Designing and teaching your sales process is behind-the-scenes work, but actually running your sales process means meeting the people.

In a global account, you will need to meet many, many people. Each single opportunity involves a large number of people; but you will be working towards dozens or hundreds of opportunities over time. In Whale Hunting, we call it "the Buyers' Table" – the configuration of people who will participate in and influence the decision to buy. It will take a major investment of time to get to know them.

Depending upon how you structure your sales team, it may be a hunter team or a farmer team opening doors. Let's assume that a hunter is responsible for opening the first door in a completely new global company.

Finding the Right Doors

As I discussed in Chapter 1, I recommend that you don't begin to meet people until you know enough about the global corporation and its strategy. Once you arm your hunter with knowledge, determine which door(s) to open first.

Of course, you want to go in at the highest level possible. Usually, that means you are trying to meet with a higher-level executive than perhaps you do with current customers. If you make a good impression on an executive, he or she may refer you to the right people, and you will have no trouble getting a meeting with them. When you succeed in getting a meeting with a well-placed executive, consider taking an executive higher than you to the first meeting.

For example, suppose you sell leadership training services. Ultimately, you will be working with an HR person to close an opportunity and to deliver it. But try to meet first not with a local HR person, but with a national or global-level person who has an interest in management development across a broad area of the company. If the company requires that you meet with procurement or with a partner company that manages their work with subcontractors, or course you need to do that. But in most cases, you will also need to meet some corporate end-users. If you can't, it's best to move on to another company or wait until policies change.

I told a story in Chapter 2 about a company that sells customer loyalty services. Typically, they work with the marketing team. But unless they have contacts and acquaintances who are more highly placed at the strategic level, their work may never really influence corporate policy. If that's the case, they are leaving money on the table with every deal.

Opening Doors

How to get in the door for the first time is beyond the scope of this book; I make the assumption that you know how to do that. Just a few caveats regarding getting in to meet a higher-level person:

- No cold calling. Find an introduction through your inbound marketing strategy, social media relationships and/ or networking

- Be prepared with sufficient knowledge and a strategic entrée. Do not talk about your product or services.

- Consider taking a peer-level executive or higher-level executive from your company with you, since your primary purpose is to introduce yourselves and talk about their business.

131

Jill offers some advice about opening the door:

> *It's a mistake to only try to get in to see one person. You need a multi-pronged approach where you try to connect with four or five people concurrently, not sequentially. Salespeople have been taught that people would be offended if they're also trying to meet with one of their colleagues—but believe me, they don't have time to talk to each other! Plus, there's such an easy way to explain it. For example, if you meet with a marketer, you simply say, "I understand that your decision affects multiple people, so I'm also talking to (or trying to talk to) your colleagues in demand gen, digital and content marketing."*

> —JILL KONRATH

When you are working in an unfamiliar culture, this entire process can be much more complicated. Greg explains that in Japan, he encountered two kinds of corporate culture:

> *One is the foreign multinational companies here who are predominantly staffed by Japanese. The president might be a foreigner, but the people we'll deal with at the execution level will all be Japanese. It's very rare we'd be dealing with someone on the execution level who's not Japanese. They're usually going to be HR people as well. The purely domestic Japanese companies are really, I would consider, old style for the most part. You are talking two different audiences.*

> *The ones that are working for the foreign multinationals tend to be a bit more modern, a bit more with it. For example, an HR person in Japan would not play the role of a partner in the business that you'd expect in an HR person in a Western company. They tend to not have that role expectation. They still play a different role to what they would play in a typical*

domestic Japanese company, but they only play that more limited role. Even though they're in a Western company they're still not operating like they would if they were in a Western environment. They're still very conservative. They're very risk averse. They worry that if they sent people to the training, and somebody complained, "Oh my God, they complained." That would be a disaster here; they are very concerned about that. They worry that they might get into trouble. "No one ever got fired for buying from IBM" was the famous television commercial in the states, right? It's that sort of mentality. Buy it from the safe and certain rather than taking a risk.

—GREG STORY

The culture also influences how you can go about meeting people in the company. I asked Greg how they go about setting a series of first-time meetings with a Japanese company?

If you sent an email here to someone that didn't know you, they didn't know your company, they'd ignore it. You send them a fax; they'll throw it in the bin. You send them a letter; they'll throw it in the bin. Straight up. They wouldn't even look at it. They don't know you, you're out. They've got to know you.

How would they know you? They're either going to know you because someone in the company was doing a search for some type of training, or because we use Google AdWords and Yahoo AdWords, and our ads will come up. They will press on that ad; it will take them to our site. They get on our site, and they then may request some white paper, or guidebooks, or report. Then we will contact them. We would ring them back and try and establish a meeting with them. That would be one route. The other options are through personal introductions or networking. Cold calling is not impossible here but it is very tough and the success rate is excruciatingly low.

—GREG STORY

You can see how different this is from Hari's process, which begins with sending out 20 or 40 letters in order to get three or four meetings. That's a difference in doing business between India and Japan.

The First Meeting

The most important sales call you will make is the first one. If your first meeting is not successful, it will be extremely difficult, if not impossible, to recover. This is the time when your first executive whale contact will decide whether you truly have a "customer mindset" as we have been discussing. If you are product-centered or focused on yourself, this meeting can be disastrous.

Each meeting is a piece of leading your customer through the buying process—some call it a journey. It's easy for me to say, "Craft a vision and lead them to achieving it," but how does that work? We've already looked at gaining knowledge about the customer and its strategy, the industry, the market, and so forth, but what does that mean in practice? Let's start with a first meeting.

Hunters and farmers and gamekeepers all have these important first meetings. There was once the first "first meeting" with an executive at this global account, but realistically you will be having a new first meeting with someone almost all the time. It's so important to come across as someone who has the right kind of approach. As a seller focused on a global account, you will be meeting what Jill Konrath called "crazy busy" executives. We asked her about what has to happen in a first meeting:

*Busy executives have a "price of admission," meaning they expect you to have done your homework. They have no tolerance for stupid questions or salespeople who talk about their products or services. To be prepared for this opportunity, look at the company, where they're going and what's happened recently. Use social media to check out the people likely to be involved in the process; see what they talk about, what interests them. Spend time looking for gaps in what they're trying to achieve or trigger events that cause priorities to shift. Then, figure out how you can help them— the difference you can make. Busy executives are always glad to meet with salespeople who bring **ideas, insights, and information** on topics of high relevance to them.*

Also, sellers have been taught to never to make assumptions. That's totally out of date. Make some assumptions! If you've worked similar companies bring your expertise to the table. It's so critical! Talk about trends, issues and challenges – as well as how others are addressing them. Discuss changing priorities. Share relevant research you've located or an insight about the trajectory of their business. "Presume" and "assume" they'll be interested in exactly what your other clients care about.

If busy executives don't find their initial meeting with you to be of value, there will not be a second meeting. Period.

You want them to say, "This is really interesting," or "We need to explore this further," or "I want to get so-and-so involved." It goes back to creating the vision.

—JILL KONRATH

Even if you are somewhat inexperienced with a large global account, you can have an outstanding meeting if you are well-prepared and completely focused on the customer. Spend some time researching their company, their industry, trends and issues common to global companies. Ask good questions about their company's strategy; ask for more explanation of interesting things you've read about them.

Ask Good Questions

Many people have written books just on the topic of how to ask good questions, and it's beyond the scope of this book. Just be sure, first of all, not to ask a stupid question. A stupid question would be one to which you should already know the answer, through your appropriate research about the company and its business. Good questions are those that arise naturally from your research and current knowledge. For example, a question about the company's corporate strategy and how it influences the role of the person with whom you're talking. A question about what's getting in the way of their path to completion. Spend some time with your team brainstorming appropriate questions to open a meaningful conversation before your first meeting.

Matt seconds the requirement for knowledge:

> I think you really have to understand your customer well. A lot of companies develop their message based way too much on what the product is and what it does. The best marketing in the world isn't product marketing; the best marketing in the world is focused on people and problems. But because you live and breathe your product, you're so proud of it all day long, it's really easy to talk too much about it. When we work with inside sales teams often we institute what I call rule number one, which is "On that first sales call, you're not allowed to talk about your product or service."

—MATT HEINZ

Matt is right: first meetings are not for selling or even for talking about your products and services. They are for getting the attention of a key person in your global account company:

> *You have to have that conversation entirely about the prospect, their issues, their challenges, what are they dealing with? If you can do that effectively, not only do you learn a lot about the prospect's situation, not only can you quickly hone in on a problem that they may or may not have quantified before. Now all of a sudden you've set the entire stage for a problem that is urgent and imminent that they need to solve.*

> *Your ability to demo your solution, first of all, is a small part of the sales process. Second of all that's more part of a close than part of the pitch. Understanding the customer well enough, and positioning your sales message and your marketing message against those early indicators of need that's unique to that buyer and their circumstance—that's what unlocks so many more conversations. This approach allows sales people to differentiate themselves and create credibility where it didn't exist before. It's not difficult to do. If you ask the right questions, prospects will tell you all day long. They want to talk about their problems, but you have to ask the right questions.*

> —MATT HEINZ

This statement is a clear testimonial to the customer-focused mindset. To achieve this kind of relationship over the long term with executive clients, put yourself aside and focus on how you can provide them with ideas and innovations and industry knowledge. Spur their thinking with carefully thought-out questions based on your current outsider's perspective of their circumstances. Ask for clarification. Ask what's working, and what isn't. Ask what's changed since their last annual report—internally or externally. Ask how something happening in another industry might be affecting their understanding.

You will meet some executives early in their careers, and as you help them succeed they will move into higher positions with greater authority. And they will bring you with them, at their first company or their fifth!

More Opportunities, More Buyers

It's just as difficult to meet all of the potential buyers when you are in the role of farmer. In fact, if you have come into the company in a small role, or if you have offered a large discount or otherwise compromised your position in order to get in the door, you may find it much harder to negotiate inside to meet new people. The new customer may pigeon-hole you as a company that only does this small business or this cheap business rather than treating you as a vendor who could become a repeat supplier and take on bigger assignments in the customer's company.

Ideally, you will come to know and preferably be working people who have a broad responsibility and especially a broad knowledge of people and positions. These are people who can and will introduce you to others that you need to meet in other parts of the company.

In some ways this is still like a brand new account because the people you are currently working with may not know the other people, and vice versa. Jill's advice still holds—you can work at the same time on meeting several people.

Approach every new opportunity from the beginning of your sales process. Each new set of buyers needs the same kind of respect and attention to detail as the very first. As you pursue new opportunities with a global account, you may have an entirely new Buyers' Table or you may have a partially new group of buyers; but whatever their composition, they will be a totally different group with different agendas than the last.

When Process Stalls

Sometimes you seem to have a good start, but during the sales process everything stalls. Maybe it stops abruptly, or maybe it grinds to a halt. Of course this is a potential problem in any kind of sale, but the large, complex sale to a global company is particularly prone to stalling. And it's all about the people:

> *What causes sales to stall? If you have the luxury to do a forensic of won and lost deals, often you can find more clues than you realize —we're going too fast, not spending enough time thinking and talking as a group, we have roles etc. but that can't substitute for dialog and strategy. It looks right on paper, but we were not talking to each other enough. Sales can fall through when the customer is ready to go, you have four weeks to prepare your proposal, but the team is not aligned. I've seen cases where an opportunity was identified months prior to receipt of the RFP. With good communication and planning a lot of work could have been done ahead of time enabling the whole team to be on board, and prepared with a strategy to win.*
>
> *Account planning should include time to develop the strategy of the deal—we all get in a hurry, but have we really all aligned and allowed for the best thinking?*
>
> —VALERIE BONEBRAKE

I have seen this countless times. An RFP or RFQ comes in with a 3-week deadline. Not only did the team know that this RFP would be coming; they have been waiting for it, maybe a year, maybe even more! But no preliminary work has been done, when in fact they could have been completely prepared for the opportunity. They could have been sketching out their approach to what they expected the customer to ask for, gathering data and proof, understanding the key needs and most important fears about this decision. Jeff explains:

My biggest concern is that deals go off track before we even realize that they've gone off track. I still have heard people of late responding when they are asked about a project that's going to be built a year and a half, two years from now, "That's going to happen way off in the future, so now I'm working on this, this and this." But I think because that other $100 million project is going to happen a year and a half from now, now is the time that we should be putting an immense amount of focus on getting in, developing those relationships, learning as much as we can while the client is still open and talking about the project, because the closer we get to the project the more that they will start to clam up in sharing a lot of the details.

I feel like we missed a lot of opportunities a year and a half out from the opportunity, and in fact when we found out that we've been outsold on some of the big jobs, part of the reason is our competitor got in to do some of the initial planning, some of the initial work, a year or a year and a half before we did.

—JEFF HARGROVES

A big part of that work you can be doing well in advance of the actual sale, or even before there is a deal on the table, is indeed getting to know all of those who will influence the decision, and in fact even helping the customer begin to understand who needs to be involved as decision-making gets closer. As Jill points out:

Research shows that 22% more decision-makers are involved today. The more troublesome it is to marshal resources in their organization, the more things get stalled out. The problem often starts with an executive who's been put in charge of fixing things, but has no experience making these kinds of decisions. The first order of business is to understand all the people, systems and infrastructure that support "how we do it here." It can often be complex, yet all this information needs to be considered before any change can be made.

Things get even more complicated—and political—when the change initiative involves organizational siloes with a vested interest in maintaining the status quo. Their work often supports the problems created by the status quo. These people certainly don't want to outsource a solution; their job is on the line if they do.

When things get hard and complicated, companies often decide to do nothing. Complexity kills decisions. It's just plain easier to stay with the status quo.

—JILL KONRATH

Jill explains that it's your job to keep the whole deal moving forward; unless you do, it will stall, predictably. The buyers typically don't know how best to organize themselves to make a buying decision. You can be the leader of that process. Reassure them that you have done this in other companies. Let them know that you can do the leg work and make it easy for them. Offer to guide and direct. Constantly work at getting more knowledge.

If an opportunity stalls before it gets off the ground or before you are too far into it, work with your team and, if possible, the buyers to decide if it's a stall or if the timing is bad all around. If a deal is not going to work now, the sooner you get out and move on to something else the better. I don't mean move out of that account, but move out of that opportunity.

Lisa identifies what she calls "the big four" reasons for account sales teams to become stalled in their long, and sometimes painful journey to secure global contracts:

- *Lack of a strong account team leader. Sometimes it is not clear, when the sales process is long and complex, who the leader is., Maybe the manager parachutes in at various times which can cause a lack of clarity. I encourage account teams to make a designation of who is the leader early in the sales process for global accounts and what are they responsible for. It seems like it should be obvious, but many times it's not. We actually added this as a short, but important step in our TOP Line Account™ System several years ago.*

- *Lack of team collaboration and clear communication. For example, the leader sends out an important email (or sets a meeting) to just a few people for a global opportunity which includes many people, instead of including the entire team. This occurs when the account leader is used to selling as a lone wolf instead of as a collaborative team player.*

- *Lack of accountability and momentum—on both sides of the table. Landing a global account generally takes many interactions over months or in some cases years. It's easy for momentum to slow, both for the prospect and the selling account team. Following the 48-hour rule™ and documenting all action items as part of the strategy brief helps maintain accountability and momentum all the way through closure.*

- *Lack of the team's understanding and willingness to prioritize strategic planning over day to day issues. Planning and account strategy work is time consuming, and prioritizing strategic account development is hard for many sales and accounts teams. A strong quarterback is the key to success.*

—LISA MAGNUSON

As you can see from Lisa's reasons, these are not practices unique to selling—in fact, the flip side of each is a core principle of good management and good teamwork on any kind of project. Why then do we seem to have less of a rigorous focus on the sales process than for the buying process?

For Jill, it comes back to patience. Salespeople, quite often being pushed by their management, have quotas to meet on a quarterly basis. Or suddenly the order comes down from on high that a certain number of purchase orders are needed within the last 2 weeks of the quarter! That alone can derail a large account sale.

> *The biggest mistake for sellers is trying to rush things. Global account clients cannot be rushed. Your and your company's eagerness to get the deal will cause you to exhibit behaviors or make offers to hopefully close it in a timely manner. But big companies don't like being rushed. You can't push a big account. Engage them and keep them moving toward their vision of the future. You will be involving all the different touch points in the account as well as your own company. You'll be cracking national boundaries into other cultures. You can't rush something like this.*
>
> —JILL KONRATH

You will progress through meetings with the many people who will influence a buying decision—even before you've identified an opportunity, you'll just be getting to know the people who operate those components of the business where your company might be of assistance.

When it's working well, your conversations will be productive, and you will ask the person you're meeting with who else you should call on, who else you should meet, and if he or she is willing to make the introduction.

If you're in a big company, you may have access to a complete support team—pre-sales, engineers, marketing, proposal development, project managers, consultants—whatever the skills are that go into running your company and delivering its products and services.

But if you are in a smaller company, you won't have a dedicated team. You'll have to learn how to borrow the resources you need when you need them. That requires having great relationships with all the business units in your company; knowing people outside of sales and building trust with them.

If you're in the company's leadership position or the sales leadership position, your best contribution is to build a culture of collaboration within your company, a culture in which everyone knows, "The village eats because we hunt."

We have heard some sound reasons why deals stall and why deals are lost. It's really instructive, as Valerie suggests, to do a careful review of lost deals to understand why you lost and what if anything you could have done better or would do differently the next time. Always ask your customer for feedback, if they are willing to share. Some companies employ a customer research company to hold these discussions with your clients, in hopes of getting honest and direct feedback.

WHALE HUNTING TIPS FOR THE BUYERS' PROCESS

Preparation. It is astonishing to hear our experts talk about how often salespeople come in to see them with little preparation except for their own product knowledge. Take the time to learn about the company, the person or people with whom you are meeting, their corporate strategy, and what's going on now.

Assumptions. Make some assumptions about what might interest your new contact, based on your research and your past experience. If you don't have much experience, talk to people at your company who do.

Ideas. Bring a key idea or two to the meeting. Not product information but outcomes information. Focus on the customer's issues and opportunities, not your own.

Relevance. A new contact will quickly escort you out if your conversation is not relevant. Learn about the person, his or her career path, and some of the challenges of their current position. If you study the corporate strategic plan (from their website or SEC filings) you can ask your new customer about how it affects their particular functional area or line of business.

Respect. In the Inuit belief system, the whale is revered. It was believed that the whale captured this year was reborn during the next spring. The whale was a gift to the village. Treat your whale customer as a gift. Show respect for their position, their time, and the complexity of their business decisions.

CHAPTER 9

BEING INSIDE

One of the first software companies that engaged The Whale Hunters was about to launch a series of new products. These products were not quite fully developed. The fundamental functions were in place, but the development team envisioned a lot of customizable features that could be built for customers, down the road.

Now this company had a rough-and-tumble sales team, rock stars every one, and focused on relationships. So they did not go out and sell the basic package, the Kia, if you will. No, they sold the Bentley – all the bells and whistles, all the bright shiny objects, all the what-ifs and nice-to-haves. Never mind that those special features didn't yet exist—the company had a long sales cycle, right? Plenty of time for Development to catch up.

It was also true in this company, again because of the independence of the sales team and its disdain for the rest of the organization, that the Project Management team could not get in and assess what the customer needed in the way of installation until after the contract was signed.

So, as you can imagine, every sale called forth a truly awful circumstance for Development, Project Management—and of course Training, Customer Service. In a couple of cases, the whale-sized customer was so angered about this state of affairs that they threatened to take our client out of business.

Doing business with global companies is unlike business you have done before, starting with what we would call a "whale attitude," expressed subtly or not so subtly by the people you encounter. Whales know that they're whales. Being a whale gives them power, leverage, and a certain kind of dominance. You have to be able to take that into account in their behavior.

Tiffani is known for saying that the most disruptive thing in the market today is actually not technology, it's the customer. Technology is not as disruptive as the customer. The customer is more disruptive because they're taking more control of the buyer journey. They're more knowledgeable when they show up. They're reaching into their own trusted network, which didn't used to be the case.

The customers have high self-esteem, genuine buying power, and a good idea of what they want long before they talk to you. They may not be correct in what they want, but they will not be easily persuaded. Their real power—the power of information, among other things— influences the whales' buying processes and preferences. You will need to position yourself as a knowledgeable and thoughtful person in order to be respected among a group of people who are well-placed, polished, and under pressure to perform at a superior level.

Let's suppose now that you have made a large sale to a global customer. You are providing services, or products with services wrapped around, and now people from your company are inside of the global customer's company installing software or delivering training or managing logistics or remediating a factory. As the sales team, you are still involved with the customer, perhaps now in an account management role, but your company's Project Manager is onsite, maybe multiple sites, and you have lots of people working for the global customer.

Here's my question to you: What kind of communication does the sales team have with the project team? Does the project team know how to learn about the client's business while they're onsite, and to send ideas forward to your sales and product development teams?

When you are doing repeated business with a global account, you will often have a team of people working onsite at the same time that the sales team is working on a separate project. Jeff's company, for example, may have a project manager with a large team working as part of the construction of a new factory. At the same time, they have a global account salesperson who is working on a new sale somewhere else in that company. That's an awesome learning opportunity for the sales team, but you have to directly build-in consultation between the sales team and the project management people who are onsite. As Jeff explains:

> Yes, that is sometimes an issue for us. We have to connect the dots. Make sure that the salespeople are aware that those people are there, and then make sure that they're meeting with them and having meaty discussions. We have even tried to pull those people into the proposal development process. If nothing else, maybe they're a project manager or more of an on the ground person, they may not even be doing anything during the proposal generation process as far as writing anything or doing physical work, but they're able to just say, "You know, I know you're thinking about doing this, but I know that the client had a problem with another company that did it that way. You may want to think about doing it thus and such instead."
>
> They're almost an in-house consultant on the project, because it can be disappointing for the client if they find out that we've gone after a project and haven't consulted with the people internally, or maybe we proposed something that they've already told somebody else in our company isn't appropriate. It can really lose a project for you. We certainly have struggled with that.

—JEFF HARGROVES

Learning on the job is another starting point for how you can really bring them something new. A new business idea, not just a new technology or solution. Valerie suggests that while you are working with a client, you are learning things that you ought to be sharing with them while your work is going on:

> *Even large mature companies that have been operating globally for a long time are still not satisfied with where they are; they are constantly looking for ways to improve processes, tools, and training. They want you to identify skill sets and attributes of your talent to help them become more successful. Pay attention to your customer's strategy, and deploy an account team that is invaluable to the customer.*
>
> —VALERIE BONEBRAKE

You become an influencer and eventually a trusted advisor by paying close attention It's not about selling. It's not specifically about your products and services. It's about bringing your perspective to bear on their business issues, whether you are the one to solve them or not.

> *The customer wants the supplier to be looking around corners for them. I am thinking about the "big data" business intelligence. How do you use this data that you collect while you are working with them, which gives you information and new ideas? Are you using what you learn to bring the new ideas to them? In my experience, this does not happen with regularity.*
>
> —VALERIE BONEBRAKE

In most kinds of businesses, especially service industries, your work with your customers provides you with priceless information about their business. In the case of Valerie's business, logistics, "big data" is generated. But all suppliers learn some kinds of things about their customers that the customers do not necessarily recognize. The customers may not ask you these things. But unless you routinely bring them new perspectives, they will not be interested in talking with you. You are vulnerable to a competitor who brings more unexpected value.

Look for Opportunities

So what can you look at, specifically, that will help you understand your customers' unstated expectations? Gerhard has some ideas:

> The top three elements that they need to look at constantly are strategy, culture and talent, and if you want to add a fourth, it's technology. The strategy has to reflect the true opportunities in the marketplace and it has to be in line with the capabilities of the organization.
>
> I think a lot of companies look at the culture and then say, "What strategy can our culture support?" Well, it should be the other way around. What is the ideal strategy and how can we change the culture and the talent to execute the strategy the best way?
>
> —GERHARD GSCHWANDTNER

As you work with a company you will learn a great deal about its strategy, culture, talent and technology. Put yourself in the habit of thinking about the interaction of these facets of their business, especially in comparison or contrast to your own experiences. You can develop your capability to lead conversations with interesting ideas and insights rather than product specifications.

You can't teach everything. But a salesperson who wants to excel can learn many things that are never part of their training. Which comes first—their intuitive insight or their desire to develop intuitive insight? I don't know. But if you want to develop those qualities in yourself, and in your team, it starts with paying close attention, all the time, in a context where you are always learning and testing whether you can apply this piece of knowledge to a problem or opportunity.

It's also a reminder that you need to nurture an account as well as you open and close each deal. You won't be great at selling to global customers unless you become exceptional at serving those customers.

> *What I've learned over the last many years is that while most of us like to believe that the client goes to competition for price, I think it's more than likely that the client goes to your competition for lack of delivery skills or lack of trust. People buy from people they know and they trust, even your client is a set of people. They have to trust your ability to deliver to your promise. I think that's the only thing that matters when you are in the service industry. That's the starting point.*
>
> —HARI SHANKARANARAYANAN

It's really a combination of what you promise and then what you deliver. Much too commonly, there is a gap between promise and delivery. The bigger the customer and the bigger the deal, the bigger the risk of a disconnect. If you are selling any kind of services into a global account, you are vulnerable.

Many of my clients sell some kind of enterprise software. They spend most of their time putting out fires related to stuff they have already sold, and they are in the midst of installing it or it's all installed but it doesn't work quite as promised. Putting out fires takes precious selling time as well as product engineering and project management and customer service and account leadership time. And it diminishes your customer's trust in you day after day.

If you are already a large company and having these problems, they will require unprecedented cooperation and collaboration among your company's functional areas. If you are a smaller company starting out with companies that do business globally, you have the opportunity to grow on both sides of the equation—the sales side and the delivery side.

I hear talk all the time about exceeding expectations—and I hear promises like that all the time. But when you are working with a global customer on a large project, many things can go wrong. It's much better to deliver more, or better than you promised, than to promise too much.

Greg identifies professionalism as the overall concept, no matter where in the world you are doing business:

> *The key to success in any market, in any industry, in any country comes down to your level of professionalism. That means being well trained in sales. It means having a back office system that is efficient, and effective, and again, professional. I think your presentation materials, your branding, your consistency of look on your website, in your physical office, in your materials, all point to a well organized business partner. For a country like Japan, that's very important. Japan is a high quality market. They will pay more for high quality; therefore, you must be high quality.*

> *How do people tell you are high quality? Well, all the touch points. If your website looks like rubbish, or your printer materials look like rubbish, or your trainer look like rubbish, then you're not going to be successful here. It forces you to be really on your game with all of those things across the board. I think on one level Japan is an extremely difficult market because of the risk-averse and hierarchical aspects of the Japanese culture, and the Japanese buyer, but on the*

flip side, like that song about New York, "If you can make it here, you'll make it anywhere," and I think Japan is a lot more difficult than New York.

—GREG STORY

A big part of exceeding expectations depends on your team's learning while they are inside working on a project. Take the time to develop clear, consistent lines of communication between project management and sales. Train your onsite operations people to share what they are observing, on a regular basis. Make a time and place for that.

Whether you are selling technology or logistics or consulting or engineering services, your customers may have a higher demand from your sales team during the buying process than the providers can actually deliver.

If you're the harpooner sitting in front of a customer, you have to be careful not to overpromise because the company isn't ready to totally deliver. You can't overpromise just in case you need partners to deliver and your partners aren't skilled. It's difficult for sellers now because of the expectations of customers as well as the rapid capability technology has given us.

That's the truth about sales and delivery. How can you be sure that the sales team is selling what the operations teams are prepared to deliver? The only way is to be fiercely focused on your customer and deliberately collaborative inside your company.

If you are small and growing, you need to have developed enough trust within your team that you can be sure you will deliver what was sold. It requires discipline and communication. It involves a team sale, where the project management team is part of the sales process, so that there are no surprises.

154

If you are large and growing, the issues of collaboration, shared knowledge, communication and trust become greater with scale. Here's where the senior management team needs to exert continual influence to maintain a customer focus throughout the company.

If you fail to keep your promises to a global account, you risk losing more than a deal. Your reputation is damaged and your future opportunities with that corporation, if any, are seriously at risk.

It goes without saying, but I'll say it anyway: you must deliver what you sell. Therefore, you must sell what your team can deliver.

WHALE HUNTING TIPS FOR BEING INSIDE

Assumptions. Assume that your global clients crave new information and thoughtful discussions about their business opportunities or threats that may have little or nothing to do with your company's services.

Training. Typical sales training programs will not teach salespeople to be exceptionally wise about the expectations of a global account. Your company needs to provide continual opportunities and mentoring, including contact with your senior management, for your sales team to learn about customers' unspoken expectations.

Industry. As you are acquiring industry knowledge and experience, pay attention to innovations in related and even unrelated industries. Some of your best ideas may come from making a connection where no one else has seen it yet.

Process. Learn as much as you can about how your global account manages its own business strategy and initiatives. The more you know, the better questions you can ask to figure out ways to become a trusted advisor.

Strategy. Align your sales strategy with your customers' corporate or divisional strategic objectives. Devote the time you need to understand what those are, how they are changing over time, and how each business unit's goals are defined by the strategy.

PROCESS SUMMARY

To manage repeat sales to global customers, you need a robust sales process focused much more on stages, or phases, than on steps. The process needs to be customized to the needs of your customers and supported with detailed documentation easily accessible to all members of an account team. You need relevant tools and collaborative roles at each phase. Pay special attention to the gaps between CRM steps that are likely to occupy months or longer of time, such as between when you first determine that there is an opportunity and when you actually make a full presentation of your solution.

Beyond the sales process, to manage a specific complex multi-million-dollar sale, there is no substitute for a well-thought out account plan which is developed with the mindset of helping customers achieve their business objectives. When you combine a strong account planning process with a robust sales process that requires a clear timeline to be established with milestones and deliverables, you position your organization and your customers for a mutually successful outcome.

PART IV

VISION: LEAD THE WAY

WHALE HUNTING PERSPECTIVES

In the world of the Inuit, the whale hunt was a sacred activity. The people held a shared vision of how the whale hunt integrated with their lives and livelihood. As I explained in my introduction to this book, the Inuit believed that the whale that they captured this year was reborn, and would return in the future. That is the vision I hold for you with your global customer: a relationship in which your customer is reborn as a consequence of doing business with you.

In an Inuit whale hunt, the harpooner sat in the bow of the boat. His job was to steer the boat close to the whale – close enough to sink the harpoon. In our modern Whale Hunting analogy, the harpooner is a salesperson, but the harpooner's job is the same—steer that boat close to the whale. Unlike some other salespeople, your harpooner has a whole team supporting him or her, in both ancient and modern versions of the story. The Inuit harpooner had seven other people in the boat to help land the whale

How do today's global account harpooners get their teams close to the whale? And how do you create the vision and convey your competence to lead? That's important in this chapter.

Whale Hunting skills are leadership skills—not simply management skills, although project management talents are helpful. Successful, long term sales relationships with global accounts are built on a vision for the future outcome that becomes shared by buyers and sellers.

CHAPTER 10

TEAM VISION

I had a once-in-a-lifetime experience at the 2000 Indy 500 when Larry and I were invited as Lyn St. James' guests. Lyn is only the second woman ever to drive at Indy, first female Rookie of the Year, and in 2000 was preparing for her final Indy 500 appearance.

We had passes to actually be in the pit, right on the track, during practice and qualifications!

I learned an astonishing thing. Lyn spent long hours just sitting in the car while her team tuned things up. Literally at a moment's notice she had to be ready to accelerate out onto the track for only a couple of laps, then come back in and talk with the crew chief and the crew in excruciating technical detail about the performance of the car. I was amazed that all of the drivers, who live for speed, had to muster up really tedious hours of readiness, sitting in full driver's suit and helmet in a tight, hot enclosure, in order to really earn the speed experience.

High-performing racing teams create speed by collaboration. The precise tuning of the chassis, the engine, the tires; the intense communication between the driver and the crew Chief; the orchestrated efforts of the pit crew. These teams prove that acceleration and collaboration go hand-in-hand.

How can you work with one global account as a complicated, dispersed team and still appear seamless?

Many people are involved in a buying decision on the customer's side, and all of those people want attention. They will want to meet some of your company's subject matter experts, not just the lead salesperson. All of the suggestions I have shared about the preparation and demeanor of the lead salesperson are equally true for other members of the team. And at some point, every member of your team is likely to have a first meeting with one of their counterparts at the whale. And then of course perhaps a second or third meeting.

A few of these meetings may be in person, but when you're working with a global account with components in many different countries, it's hard to manage face-to-face meetings. You have inside salespeople, and perhaps one of them has opened the door to your first or the subsequent next deal. There are so many possible scenarios of how you get in the first time or two or three, but soon, in order to land a big deal with a whale, you will undoubtedly involve other players from your company's team.

There has to be a team to serve a global account. In Valerie's experience:

> *We always used a team approach. The Business Development leader delivered sales proposals. We had an engineering or design team, a pricing analyst, an operations leader, technology, overall project management, and a technical writer from marketing. The partnership between operations and sales was critical because ultimately operations had P&L responsibility. The role of technical writer is increasingly important to tell the story, provide supporting documentation without giving away the solution, and create the right graphics for an impressive proposal.*

> —VALERIE BONEBRAKE

As Valerie describes, you have to have multiple people involved. What differs from one company to another, or one deal to another, is how closely this team collaborates during the entire process or is only pieced together when it's time to write a proposal or respond to an RFP. The most successful companies follow a deliberate sales process that reminds them how to include representatives of each of the important roles long before the proposal is needed, far ahead of the presentation, before the need appears to the customer.

Bigger companies may have an entire team dedicated to the account. Melissa distinguishes here between the overall relationship with a global account and the specific opportunities as they arise:

> *We work as a team. Depending upon where we are in the sales cycle, we include at a minimum a Global Account Director and a Global Sales Director on each account to manage the ongoing relationship. As we move into an opportunity sale cycle, we will include various pre-sale people, members of our consulting organization, product development, legal and finance teams as needed to become part of the combined pursuit team. We include anyone needed to drive the success of the overall opportunity including our Executive team.*

—MELISSA DONNELLY

For Melissa, working in a large company, at least two people are managing the customer relationship. They bring other employees into the mix whenever there is a specific opportunity for a sale. It's a formal process, with pre-sale employees and product group employees and consulting group employees available to become part of a team.

The subject matter experts on an Ingram Micro sales team come from different sources, but they are available to work with the sales-people on specific accounts, as Kirk explains:

We have a strong bench with a world-class tech team, pre-sales support, and pre-sales engineers. SMEs for solution sales are typically employees of Ingram but some with vendor funding. The larger vendors have large teams funded by the vendor. They all get involved with the sales process, specifically when it is technical. They have teams that handle pricing and bidding, a classic sales team responsible for that business.

—KIRK ROBINSON

Even with a great deal of support, putting a team together and then leading the team to make a large account sale takes a lot of work and coordination, over and over again.

Leadership

It sounds and looks graceful, but like Gerhard's swans, people are churning under the surface. It's a big job to manage the inner workings of setting up the sales team for a new opportunity because the available resources are not dedicated to one deal or one company but move into and out of deals as needed.

The hardest part of all is to maintain the cooperation and collaboration among all of the people who need to be involved—all of the buyers and all of the necessary people on the sellers' side. It requires negotiation, sharing, and accommodating others so that your entire company wins.

And that means a team vision. But these may be team members with much different responsibilities, various methods of compensation, multiple other work obligations pulling at them while they are also working on a deal. How do they become a team?

First, teamwork has to be a core competency and high value in your company. As the company founder, CEO, or president you must lead in promoting a culture of collaboration; that direction has to come from the top. Many people are afraid that collaboration on a project slows everyone down and leaves too much room for some employees to slack off. However, in my experience and in the words from my expert contributors, collaboration as a team is the core requirement for selling a big deal into a global account.

As the global sales leader, you need to encourage and support the entire management team in fostering a collaborative culture. Your team will need help from many cross-functional areas at one time or another, as you need to borrow other people to be on the boat for a particular deal. Making that happen requires deliberate level of trust and collaboration.

As the sales person or account manager for a global account, you are the harpooner—the leader of a particular sale. You will need to practice leading a diverse team of people who do not report to you, people over whom you have no authority. Being able to do that requires that participants buy in to the deal and they buy in to you. They will help you create and elaborate upon and then implement the vision that you are all holding for the customer.

How does it work for a smaller company? You can't afford to have many people on the bench—maybe none at all. However, it may be easier to maintain a collaborative culture, since that is what supports your ability to grow. Here's how Rachel has managed:

> I think the one thing that I'd say is that for a salesperson selling into a global account, the best thing that you can do is put more people in your boat, including executive sponsors. What I see from my less successful sales reps is that they are close to the vest. I think they're probably afraid of being scrutinized or getting inspected throughout the deal cycle.
>
> One of the things I've always done and all of my best salespeople have done is include people in the boat, get

different opinions, triangulate. The more people that you can seed into the account, the more ideas you have, the more touch-points you have, the better the chance of success is for the deal. For me the secret to success is to be prepared, put a whole team in place and share information, really listen to your customer, understand their business and build a good relationship.

—RACHEL BARGER

When you know what success requires, it's easier to build the cooperative spirit into your company and into your deals.

Gerhard suggests that technology challenges at the enterprise level require a great deal of teamwork within the selling company. Whether you are selling technology solutions or something else, the technology already in use in your global customer's organization will dictate many decisions:

Another big change is that technology is like the tower of Babel. There are many languages spoken, and there is a lot of simultaneous talk going on, meaning that somebody may be on a saleforce.com platform in sales, and they may use Oracle CTQ to deliver posts, and they may have in the back end an ESP system from SAP. There is no single language spoken in technology in any company.

It's difficult to create something that's unifying because everybody wants to optimize but there is no one system that can do everything.

It adds a layer of complexity to every organization, and if you are a vendor to a big organization like that, you're dealing with a level of complexity that requires a team of sellers and a team of buyers. Then you need to align their schedules and get everybody on the same page, which means that sales processes become much longer because of the shifting priorities and the lack of availability.

—GERHARD GSCHWANDTNER

Global accounts present immense complexities as well as immense opportunities. Gerhard's example illustrates how complicated things are for the people that you're selling to, as well as your own team. As you gather a sales leadership team on your side, you'll also be finding and recruiting leaders on the customer's side who will be helping you move the vision ahead.

The international aspects of a global customer certainly come to bear in the process of a specific deal. The buyers' team may be multicultural, as may your team, so you have to get the details right.

As you go into new markets to understand their culture to understand their etiquette, there is no detail too small that you can leave out because sometimes something little will demonstrate you don't understand their business, you don't understand their culture, you don't understand local customs and traditions and that's important. I think that goes for everything, from the way you sell, to the way you service customers, to the way the product is localized.

—MATT HEINZ

Even when your company is strongly committed to providing all of the supporting team that a global deal requires, it's still not easy to get all of the technical people involved when you need them:

It's always a challenge because there's a lot of activity and we don't have a lot of people sitting idle. Some solutions are hotter than others, so the work load varies and it is often a juggling act. To properly manage each opportunity to assure we have the right coverage at the right time, we've developed a process as part of the overall sales methodology. The goal is to manage opportunities and assure that we've qualified them properly so we have the right resources at the right place at the right time.

—MELISSA DONNELLY

To practice collaborative leadership and team selling in global accounts requires a serious commitment from within your organization. It requires confidence in your team and willingness to take a long-term view. Most important, it requires that corporate leaders, sales leaders, and global salespeople exercise leadership skills for a team vision at every level.

Preparation

Once you have a sales team put together, as the sales manager or harpooner you may need to help them get ready to be in front of the customer on a call or in a presentation. When your company is new to the process, and your SMEs don't have much experience in working with you on a global account sale, you need to provide them with ways to learn what's expected of them.

Every call should have a plan, and every team member should be involved in rehearsing. Especially if you don't know each other well, you will need sufficient time to plan.

Preparation is a key element of your team vision for a client. There's a big difference between "getting ready" for a presentation and "orchestrating a vision." Great sales leaders take part in rehearsals and presentations and use opportunities for training all the time: As Rachel explains:

I do a lot of modeling with the team. I'll say, "Why don't we do a ride-along together," but also try to let them do their part. Do a lot of prep. As an example, we've done three prep calls on an executive briefing we're going to do for a customer on Tuesday because it is a critical meeting to unlock future opportunities and gain his sponsorship. It's the sales leader's responsibility to make the time to do prep with their team and to review. That's the best way for them to learn, because it's practical, and then they know that you're there with them when they need you and what your expectations are.

You can't do it all the time, but you have to pick those important moments to do it. Then get them to help train each other and do inspection with each other. That's one of the things I try, to get my teams working a lot together and talking to each other together so they start using each other to bounce ideas off of and doing dry runs of messaging together.

The big thing that I focus on with everybody is pay attention and read the room, read the situation. So many times, people get so caught up telling their story that they talk over people and miss really important opportunities to learn more about their prospect or their business. Take the time to listen. Really, really listen. Watch the room and watch people's eyes when they're not into it, then move along. Just some simple things like that, to take best advantage of the prep work that they have done.

—RACHEL BARGER

Rachel is highly committed to continual education and practice with her team. It's easy for a team to short-change their preparation—especially a new team put together to present the components of a larger project.

WHALE HUNTING WITH GLOBAL ACCOUNTS

It pains me to see a deal lost at the presentation stage. You've been working towards a global account sale for more than a year; the proposal is in-house and you've been selected to make your presentation in person. Your team is geographically dispersed, so you're coming together at the last minute from multiple places. Someone is late—and because of that may be rude. You rehearsed by going through your PowerPoint on the phone, but you only talked "about" what each was going to say—there's really no script. You didn't rehearse answers to the difficult question they might ask. You didn't discuss who would really orchestrate the meeting, because of course these people don't all report to you!

And guess what—your "bunch of people" lost to a "well-rehearsed team."

This work calls for an immense store of leadership, and everyone who is a leader during the process needs to be exercising the appropriate leadership skills—from the top and across the organization. If you lose a deal because of a weak presentation, or a critical mistake of some kind, or someone is too tired or being cranky, or one of you is underprepared, you may have lost thousands of dollars or even millions of investment into the opportunity—not to mention the value of the business that you didn't get.

To counteract the problem of insufficient team preparation, a global account team can work together on a large account in the "war room." This method defines the team from the onset of an opportunity not just at the last phases. Lisa frequently leads her clients through a war room experience for a particular deal:

> *"War Room" is a concept. With a global account team, it is usually a virtual room. The entire team will come together bringing experience and preparation—everything that is needed to dive into an account and map out the strategy. They may be dealing with all aspects at one time or some*

specific components such as relationship mapping or a competitive analysis. It's so important to have the right kind of preparation and experience to think about an opportunity as well as a system to help the entire team think and act strategically. If you bring this kind of focus, the chances of missing anything are low.

Multi-million dollar accounts require the same effort as a war effort – both tactically and strategically. However, it's more than worth it! They are transformational for your company. They provide a revenue stream over a long period of time, they become reference accounts, and they offer a template for future global accounts and provide stable revenue for needed, investments. Some will become banner accounts, opening doors for your company that were previously locked. There are so many positive aspects to landing a TOP Line Account™; it's worth every bit of the time and attention required. The War Room is a proven structure that works.

Senior sales leadership needs to direct the sales team in a war room effort. They are most productive when there is lots of preparation. For example, usually there is a core team—the account leader, their manager, one or two other people—who get together prior to the war room event to think about and plan for the who, what and why associated with the workshop.

A successful war room session strikes a balance of structure, creativity, and flexibility. One essential aspect of structure that's usually missing is to write down the agreed upon tactics, the points of what we are going to do, who's going to do them, and by when. It sounds so basic but unless someone drives it, you cover the same territory the next time you get together. It's helpful to bring in an expert for clarity, focus, and accountability. For those companies who have good automation and technology (a robust CRM with integrated sales enablement tools), it really enhances the strategic account planning process.

—LISA MAGNUSON

From technical and solution design support, to pricing analysis and product specifications, to project management and operations, the sales people who work on global accounts need to become superb team leaders and talent orchestrators. Nowhere is this more important than in their relationship with the marketing arm of their company. If you have any gaps or lack of understanding or cooperation between your sales and marketing teams and their leaders, you need to start today to change that organizational culture. If not, you will be left behind by savvier companies that are blending these functions seamlessly in the service of their customers.

Leading the Channel

When you really bring a sales organization to the largest scale, leadership requirements multiply exponentially. Take for example introducing a new product, with a new method of delivery, and a new method of pricing when you are selling through a channel, as Tiffani discusses:

The sales process is no longer linear, it's fluid, and driven by the customer and not the sales rep. Many sales leaders feel they can't move their own sales organization as fast as customers demand, so how do you expect me to move 10, 20, 30, 40,000 partners whom I don't own that fast?

For example, Microsoft has 350,000 partners globally, many of which are managed by IT Wholesale distributors like Ingram Micro, Tech Data and Avnet. Do you think they can go, "We're just going to start selling Office 365 today and we prefer you sell this over the on premise version you have been selling for 20 years" and everyone goes, "Okay"? It's been a five-year journey for them to move those partners from Software and services to BPOS to O365 and its still a journey. It takes time to transform an ecosystem, regardless of its size, because you don't own the resources outright. You can only motivate them to want to change using various incentives and growth incentives.

—TIFFANI BOVA

Whether you are near the beginning of your global account journey or you are responsible to manage 25,000 direct sellers and 350,000 partners for Microsoft, you have to lead. Prepare. Do whatever it takes to build efficient, effective teams.

What will it take for YOU to lead the best global account team in the world? From any point in the process, you can be a leader as well as supporting and encouraging others to lead. I know a company whose leadership motto is "the leader is whoever knows what to do next." That's likely to be a different person at different decision points. Build a structure that rewards collaboration, preparation and leadership.

WHALE HUNTING TIPS ON THE TEAM VISION

Integration. Complex sales to complex global companies require an unprecedented level of functional integrations throughout your company. These should resolve into powerful, cross-functional sales teams and account management teams for your named accounts. The integration of sales and marketing leads the way in new corporate B2B strategies.

Collaboration. Perhaps the most important principle that I learned from studying the Inuit whale hunters is the incredible level of collaboration required to carry out a successful whale hunt. Everyone has a role, and all roles are equally important. Build a collaborative culture in your company—or if you can't affect your whole company, at least build a collaborative culture within each sales team.

Orchestration. The harpooner (salesperson) and the shaman (sales manager) are responsible for orchestrating the talent in their boat (selling team). Rather than doing everything herself, the salesperson will need to coordinate all of the relationships, contacts, and promises between the members of her team and the whale's team. If this is not your strong suit or if it's a new role for you, seek out some team leadership training.

Feedback. Not everyone on the team is in a client-facing position. Those who are must be devoted to providing feedback about the client to other team members who work more behind the scenes. Unless everyone is kept informed about the client, the team will be hampered in its operation, and is subject to losing out to better-informed competitors.

CHAPTER 11

THE BUYERS' VISION

I had a great engagement with a company that made soil treatments to control dust. Literally, they could treat the unpaved driveway up to your house in New Mexico, or they could treat a make-do desert helicopter landing site in Afghanistan. And they did both.

They shipped to many places in the world, by train and by freighter. Semis and train cars full of their magic substances were going everywhere. They had started to manufacture in Europe. For a small company, they were growing globally, fast.

I organized a whale hunting workshop for their entire team—at the time, about 30 people. Everyone in the company, whatever their role, was included.

They worked in teams on the Target Filter™ exercise, and each team reported out to the group about their definition of an ideal customer. Two guys from the warehouse won the day when they drew their line in the sand—"No more pails."

"If we can ship truckloads, train car loads, and ship loads, we have to stop selling this stuff in little quantities. It's too expensive and it takes too much time away from our bigger obligations. No more pails!"

Shortly after that workshop, I visited their new website—featuring military helicopters on the home page. No more driveways – no more pails!

Although this company had made inroads into some military installations, and they had a contract or two with major municipalities to provide the substance that would treat the shoulders of newly-paved roads, they had resisted actually doing the application themselves. Their business model was to create, package, and ship the necessary quantity of the soil-treatment substance and train the end users to apply it with their own equipment.

A number of customers wanted a "done for us" solution, however, and employees in the planning workshops became a voice for the customer: "We have to do this."

They were already presenting a vision—for example, to a US army general in Afghanistan and his procurement team—that if they treated the desert landing pads for helicopters, the army could control the dust that a helicopter kicked up before landing, thereby greatly reducing the number of crash landings caused by the dust interfering with the pilot's sight. But they didn't want to deliver the whole vision—they wanted to ship stuff and teach the Army how to apply it. It was less expensive and more functional, they thought. But their customer just wanted it done. All done. And other customers wanted the same thing. So, they altered the business model and began to provide the complete service.

Create the Vision

Maybe you've been in sales or sales management for a long time. But if you've recently moved into a named account role, having worked on smaller accounts previously, you will find yourself in a whole new world with a whole new role. As Jill explains:

176

*The biggest change is learning how to move from a salesperson to a business leader—a huge shift. It's not about selling anymore; **it's about creating a viable vision** with your clients about what's possible by changing. You have to hold the vision during the entire time it takes the account to make a change. And it takes forever.*

Global account sales is a business leader's job, which implies you have to have a lot more business acumen than you had before. You have to be really good at influence skills. Since you have no direct control over so many people, you have to continue to help them understand why it is to their benefit to keep moving forward. It takes great patience.

You also need to influence people in your own company to invest time working with you on the change initiative. Often, you'll want them to do something that eats up their time, but they don't get compensated for it. Sometimes it's even harder to do this in your own organization than with a client.

—JILL KONRATH

Typical sales training focuses on discovering the customer's vision or probing for relevant problems. But that presumes that customers know what outcomes they can achieve, know what it will take to achieve them, and know how to build enough consensus in their company to make a big change possible.

But in large part customers don't know those things. They are better at identifying problems than in visualizing outcomes, but you are the expert in what's possible. As Jill suggests, you need to identify all the people in the customer's company and in your company who need to come on board. You'll need to set up the meetings or conversations, bring the right people together when necessary, learn who is just taking up your time rather than contributing to the process, and do all of this repeatedly.

Forrester Research reported that 65% of the time, executives give preference to the seller who sets the buying vision. That's an enormous advantage, but typically a salesperson has not been taught that her role is to create and hold a vision for the customer's company or division over a long period of time (maybe 18 months, maybe much longer) and how to influence all of the relevant people at her own company as well as the global account company.

If "the vision thing" makes you uneasy—sounds a little airy-fairy perhaps—let me bring it down to solid ground. A major part of your vision is the path that you will take to put it into place. That's when, and why, you have to be the leader. In a big sale to a global account, things will stall. People move around, they have competing priorities, budgets get cut or postponed. The buyers know this. Perhaps your champion is afraid of all the work it will require or all the possibilities for error.

> *Craig Elias talks about prospects who have a need but have not yet explored solutions. It's one of those situations where they know they have a problem but either they don't know how big it is or they don't know where to go or they don't know that solutions exist. Those are prospects that are not explicitly seeking solutions. They're not Googling your brand, they haven't yet done the translation between the problem they have and the fact that there may be a solution out there.*
>
> —MATT HEINZ

Let's go back to those military personnel who are involved in combat or a peacekeeping operation in mountainous or desert country. They won't be building any permanent paved landing platforms for the helicopters, but the vehicles have to land. Chances are the leaders don't know there is a solution to that problem. When you approach them, you need to begin to craft the full vision of their potential outcome—fewer crashes, fewer lives lost. They already want the outcome; they don't know that it's achievable until you come along.

Preparation

Perhaps it is a general or someone in high command who is the first to share your vision for what can happen—in this case saving lives. It's not the general's job to figure out with you how to make that happen; many other people will have to be involved in detailed processes. You will need to become expert in managing the buying process to implement the vision you've held up for the leaders.

It's not about your product or your service or your company. It's rather about painting the picture of a future outcome that the buyers can rally around; they can become so desirous of achieving that outcome that they will accept and even welcome your leadership to make it all happen.

You can't just buy training to learn how to create a vision for someone else's future! Knowledge, experience, maturity and coaching will help you to get there. But while you're acquiring this kind of wisdom, it will help to have a robust team of fellow whale hunters who can bring their experience and ideas to the process. You can't manufacture maturity. But even if you are quite young in your harpooner role, or you are responsible for managing a young team, be responsible to have industry experience, market knowledge, influence, and maturity in your boat, on your team.

I've talked about the buyers' process, but rarely is it a clear path to those buyers who are the end users. If you have set an outcomes vision for end users, and now they share your vision, they will need you to lead the way. Long before procurement gets involved with a specific kind of request to fulfill, internal sponsors need your help to accomplish the vision. As Jill explains:

Another thing you have to learn is how to become a guide to this process. Literally you need to use your expertise with other large global accounts—to direct what comes next. You'd be paying attention to the various stakeholders that need to be engaged – and when. Based on your experience with other companies, you might, for example, choose to bring legal in early rather than later since they always have show-stopping opinions.

Smart global account salespeople will be the orchestra leaders, telling the client "We have experience working with companies like yours making these decisions." They know their job is to make clients feel like they're in the good hands of someone who has done this before. They need to shepherd clients, warn them, and get to the results sooner.

Salespeople must guide the process, and they're not used to doing that. They're used to letting customers lead. Most salespeople have no idea how to be the guide. Nor do they understand the sheer relief on the client's side when someone else takes the lead. Clients don't want 62 options—they just want the plan. They want you to reduce risk, warn them of any potential pitfalls and ensure a good investment.

—JILL KONRATH

According to Jill, it's like your personal financial planning. Most people don't want to know all the detail on all the funds and all their options. Let a skilled advisor help you determine your objectives and then figure out the strategy and portfolio that will best achieve them. Then you only have to decide how much to invest!

Of course, there are significant cultural differences among buyers in different countries. As Greg observes:

In a Japanese context, because their sales people are not trained, their buyers are also equally untrained in the sales process. What I mean by that is, a very typical Japanese buyer meeting would run along these lines: "Okay, come in here and give us your pitch. We will then tell you what's wrong with it, and you can then leave." That's the typical Japanese buyer approach. They expect you to come in, show them your stuff, they'll tell you what's wrong with it, then you can go.

That's not our process. Our process is we want to ask questions to fully understand their needs, and make sure if we've got a solution that matches their needs. To ensure that we can properly explain how that works, we need to ask questions. But the thought of a vendor, the thought of a sales person asking questions of the buyer, that's probably, "Wow, how impertinent"

If you just start plowing in, and asking questions they think you're rude, and an upstart. A "how dare you" type of attitude. You don't get much cooperation. In a Western environment, the request to ask questions would not be such a big deal. Probably there isn't even a request to ask questions. You probably just start asking questions. But in a Japanese environment, we teach that you have to get permission to ask questions.

It might be something along these lines: "In Japan we offer a broad range of services. For example, there's a luxury brand here out of Italy. We trained every single person in their entire sales area on the shop floor, and their managers told me they had a 30% increase in sales in the subsequent year. Maybe, we could do something similar for you, I'm not sure. In order for me to understand if that is possible, would you mind if I asked you a few questions?" That would be a very compressed version of what we would say.

—GREG STORY

It's not that you wouldn't try to develop a vision with your Japanese customers. It's just that you would have to approach it much differently, even diffidently. The vision in the previous example is "30% increase in sales" one year later. But it would be considered arrogant of you to approach that directly.

Every culture has its own norms for doing business, for the role of a seller and the role of a buyer. For the nature of a business relationship. For the appropriate degree of distance or intimacy. You have to learn from people in the country how to respect their customs. Don't make the mistake of seeing "Asia" as a market, for example, instead of each individual country. There are enormous differences among Japan and China or Russia or India.

Gaining Insight

If you've been in a global account sales role for a while, then you've seen significant changes in your customers' buying behaviors, preferences, and needs. Not only do you need to be able to create the vision for your large customers, you need to offer insights about their business. Gerhard explains:

> It's all a question of insight, and what is the definition of insight? It's that you understand the cause and effect based on what you're observing, whether you're observing relationships or markets or behaviors or what is the local context and what is the global context.
>
> Insightful sales people then make it their mission to see an existing client problem in a new way or connect the existing problem to another cause that's external or internal, or see the problem through the eye of a solution they had implemented with another client, or draw on their past experience. They look at an existing problem and see a pattern that shows a larger coherent context, a larger image.

Demonstrating insight is not only a tactical challenge but also a strategic challenge, and insight always needs to go hand in hand with innovation. Innovation is the twin of insight.

—GERHARD GSCHWANDTNER

Insight into the situation prepares you to create something new, to actually craft that vision for your customer. That's where great ideas come from. Not out of the blue, but within a context of having new insight on an existing situation. It might be a problem or an opportunity for an improvement that hasn't yet been thought of or drawn up or written down. You and your team can become the innovators based on new insights into your customer's business.

To acquire insights, you need a constant awareness of what's new in business, not only in your own company and your customers' companies but in general. What are the new technologies, the trends? Do you understand what's happening in supply chain trends? What's happening in HR? What's happening in finance transformation? What's happening in positioning new product sets in the newer markets? What are the best trends happening in an enterprise manufacturing space or a logistics and distribution space, or a compliance and risk space?

The ability to synthesize goes a long way in developing insight. Bring disparate ideas or data points together to form a coherent whole. Simply looking at things side-by-side that are usually separate can do the job. Your role as either hunter or farmer in a global account is to become a sort of internal consultant for specific issues that are or may be related to your company's products and services.

Breaking Barriers

The peripheral knowledge that your team acquires will sharpen your ability to become innovators, to provide insights to your customers—ideas for outcomes that they haven't yet imagined or that they don't know how to achieve.

Wherever, whatever product line I've sold, I've always focused on selling into big, complex accounts. If it's a fresh account, then you can really paint a vision. There are a lot of different stakeholders but you manage those stakeholders and you paint a vision and you move forward and if you've found the right target and done your homework hopefully you sell them on your vision.

With an install base account, using a land and expand model or trying to get a big deal going as an upsell, there can sometimes be a lot of old baggage that you have to work through especially with technology sales. How is the product working; are they using it the right way? You really have to invest a lot of time, I think, to make sure that the customer is using what they bought from us well and getting the most out of it. Only then can we really inspire them to buy more, to take a chance and believe our vision, because we've shown them what is possible.

We recently did that with a strategic customer in Europe. Sometimes it takes a change of stakeholders or sometimes you really have to do some thorough account planning to re-engage with executive sponsors, because you can get caught further down in the accounts over time. How do you plan the account to get yourself up and talking to the people who will have the vision to break down some barriers? That's probably the biggest frustration, getting through that phase so then you can actually start working on crafting a mutually beneficial deal.

—RACHEL BARGER

What Rachel explains is the typical course of events within a global account. You hope to acquire a continual stream of new business throughout the lifetime of your relationship with this customer. So there will always be existing outcomes that you have attempted to provide, and the better you have done the last one, the more likely you are to garner agreement to go ahead with another. But you will not be operating in a vacuum; the past and perhaps current circumstances surround you and your company.

The buyers' consumer experience also influences B2B experience. Transitioning to the Cloud, for example:

> *"When I go to work, I can't use Dropbox. I need to share my file with Sally. Why can't I just share my file with Sally with Dropbox?"*

> *"You can't use Dropbox."*

> *"Okay, well, if I can't use Dropbox, what can I use?"*

> *"You can't use anything."*

> *"Why can't I use any thing?"*

All the things we take for granted on the consumer side are not yet replicated on the B2B side. Many companies are slow to resolve legal and security issues of cloud computing or fear their employees' use of social media.

20 years ago, not everyone had a desktop at their home or a smartphone in their hand. Salespeople could craft and shape the message to them about what technology meant and how it could help their business, whereas today people's expectation of technology comes not only from their work experience but from their consumer experience. It's harder because of the legacy infrastructure in the US.

But this circumstance is highly subject to differences in cultural experience.

Outside the US it's a very different story. In the US, people went from land line phones sharing in a neighborhood, to everyone having a land line phone, to call waiting, to some clunky cellphone to smartphones. In emerging markets, they skipped all that innovation and went right to the power of a smartphone!

If you are working in newer markets, you won't have to deal with legacy systems—a real advantage. But if your mobile sales and marketing and logistics and technology systems are not world class, you will be at a distinct disadvantage.

To manage your role as a global account salesperson demands exceptional knowledge and preparation, as Jill says:

> *Qualities that promote success are business acumen far beyond sales knowledge. Moving to a global account is a real shift in mentality for a sales rep. It's the same as moving from a sales rep to a sales management position. There are so many moving parts: it's moving to a division leader, managing and working with people in a whole different way. Because decisions are so slow, it's about continuously bringing value to clients, always thinking about helping them get better over time.*
>
> *Global account sellers need a maniacal focus on making a difference – for their client! So much so that people in their own company complain that they are too into their customer's business! But that's how they should be. The truth is, when you're dealing with global accounts you can't work with too many of them because of your in-depth focus.*
>
> —JILL KONRATH

I have worked with companies where global account salespeople worked with ten accounts, or five accounts, or three accounts, or occasionally only one account! As your business with global accounts expands, you will find yourself devoting increasing resources to each one. Then you also have to manage the P&L, to be sure that your margins keep up with the higher cost of sale.

Think of Kirk's problem: "solve the global trade issues." Solve something that's an issue for the customer! When you are assigned to a named account, you have endless opportunities to learn from your customers if you ask pertinent, relevant business questions and pay attention to their answers. When your mission is to craft a vision for your buyers, you have more likelihood of being engaged with them because you will have interesting conversations—not about your company or your services or your products but about their strategic business issues. Hunt for insights, and sales will follow.

It's another reason why marketing needs to be on your team.

> *You're not looking for leads; you're not trying to set up a paid search campaign to get attention. You can figure out who the people are that you need to talk to. A good marketing team is going to arm their sales organization with insights about the business and about the customer. What's the angle you should be taking to engage in a need analysis discussion with that prospect? What are the trigger events and buying signals that may have recently occurred that have changed the conditions of that company that made a "nice to have" into a "need to have?" What are the signals you're identifying and leveraging and how are you leveraging those to position yourself as an enabler of achieving the results that may have just become a priority for that customer?*
>
> —MATT HEINZ

It's not the harpooner's responsibility to know everything. It's his job to keep the boat close to the whale, coordinate the knowledge and skills of the larger team, and bring them into the appropriate contact with their counterparts on the whale's buying team.

I asked Kirk what he thought was his team's potential for growing more of the reseller companies the way they have grown a handful. He shares a vision with his customers, but the end vision that they want to achieve does not come easily, as he also explains to them:

> There's a lot of upside because of the sheer amount of end users as the world becomes flat – the end users are springing up all over the world and the resellers are keeping up with that trend.
>
> But even the resellers are all different. They have different vendor authorizations. They have different appetites for whether they are willing to go set up in another region. We can help any customer understand how to do global sales, but it's not solved because we still have to work with the vendors to get them to understand how to give that authorization. You do it one off but it's not easy. Can we get the major vendors to say "Here's how we're keeping products flowing through the world?"
>
> We work on both sides, really attuned to the needs of the customer. We are up front with the customers who want us to make it simple: we can get them there but it will be painful for them to get there.
>
> It makes for a complex sale. The accounts we're having success with – $6 billion accounts or $100 million or even $50 million companies – once they understand how to go to market in a region and they're having success, that's when they can go in and sell more to the end user. But they're in for a bad

conversation about how long it will take. Once they understand, they can go for deeper penetration of that customer.

—KIRK ROBINSON

More Learning

Kirk is in a new business—the business of bringing his reseller partners up to speed on how to sell to global accounts. It's not all put together, and maybe no one has yet figured out the nuances of how to get these new services paid for. But it's a whole new business for many companies.

It's not only technology companies that have these sales distribution challenges. In today's world, big deals are usually a combination of service and product, or they are service alone. Even in product companies a great deal of service is required in order to fulfill all of the supply chain expectations. Most deals involve technology somewhere along the line; someone else's technology if not yours. The concept of global accounts simply adds more dimensions to an already complex set of problems to solve, and opportunities to master.

Closely related to developing this ability to create a vision for your customer through insight is your ability to learn, as Jill explains:

Another quality is learning agility—the ability to pick things up fast, to spot changes early and to take action on them. For example, do you have perceptivity about people and trends? Don't continue to be going down the path you were on when you perceive changes. Successful salespeople are continually using their brain. Thinking and learning, adjusting and readjusting.

—JILL KONRATH

Gerhard talked earlier about the speed of business, such that the decisions made 12 months ago and not yet implemented may be hopelessly out of date already! This is what makes selling to global accounts really exciting—the continual challenge to learn and use your learning quickly to your customer's advantage and to the advantage of your account team. And what kind of person does that require? Sid suggests:

> It's really important to take the time to carefully listen and understand what business challenges and pain points the organization is facing. Through active engagement and regular dialogue, help your customer understand the possibility of solutions and help them come to their own conclusions as to the best course of action. A product-led discussion will not work. But a product and solution conversation is the natural endpoint as you discuss a customer's business challenges and pain points.
>
> In this digital world, information is abundant and virtually free. A strong salesperson needs to be much more consultative and help solve business problems. He or she needs to be a good listener, a problem solver, and a partner.
>
> —SID KUMAR

Of course, in order to craft a vision for your client you need to do a great deal of listening and learning. Traditionally, however, salespeople are taught how to talk—what to say, what to demonstrate, how to master the product knowledge. But that is not the way to lead a global account:

> The ability to listen to somebody and listen to the story behind the story like a journalist doesn't come easily because sales people want to shine, they want to persuade, they want to influence, they want to sound brilliant and bright and the

creation of insight is more a product of listening and reflection than talking, and I don't know many insightful talkers.

—GERHARD GSCHWANDTNER

If your salespeople are trained primarily on the features and benefits of your services, what they will know primarily is how to talk about your company during the sales process. But unless they learn first, why they should be listening instead of talking, and second, how to direct questions that will allow the customer to do the talking, they will continue to make the mistake that Gerhard identifies.

Incumbents

Always there are two tensions during the buying process—one which makes it hard for a new company to break in to a global account, and another which makes it hard for an incumbent to stay on top.

It usually boils down to the contrast among salespeople. One is the incumbent, who knows that his company has a fully-developed product that has been renewed for many years and therefore believes that no competitor can come up with a more highly developed product, so why would the customer switch? Another has been trying for quite a while to break into this account, but because his company's software isn't really any better than the competitor's, he does not devote a lot of time to this particular renewal sale, regardless of its size. Both of these seem to accept the status quo with this customer.

But along comes another kind of salesperson, one who continually discusses ideas and insights with the customer's IT team and is always on the lookout for a new differentiator. If that salesperson works for a fast-growth company, she may help her product people come up with the innovations.

191

Or the incumbent team will not take for granted an automatic renewal; in fact, will work hard to continue to add more value in innovative ways.

How did desktop printers become scanners and fax machines and digital workshops? Because customers and customer service reps and salespeople and product people asked "what if" and "why not?"

Bring Your Insights Home

The product development team is not in contact with the client in the same way that the sales team is. A company whose sales team is extremely well-versed in their global customer's business and continually on the lookout for ideas and observation will have a significant competitive advantage.

Two of the people whom I've interviewed for this book—Hari and Rachel – were members of the APAC sales team for a company called Ariba when I worked with them on whale hunting practices in 2008. Ariba was a small global company that did so well, it was acquired by SAP. I asked Hari what were some of the sales practices that made Ariba so successful?

> *I think there were multiple things that we did at Ariba. As you can imagine, we were a fairly small company with a small team, but the difference between large corporate team and Ariba was that everyone was at all points of time wired in to what was happening both locally and globally in the organization and shared a lot of information on a regular basis across industries, across companies, across geographies. What we did well, as far as the sales process was concerned was the fact that almost all the folks on our sales teams understood the product and the offering well.*
>
> *If you spoke to three different Ariba folks, one from Australia, one from India, and one from the United States, you would*

find them describing the product in a similar fashion. It would be different terminologies that were localized to the market, but the feature functions covered and the value described of the products were always consistent. We were well trained on understanding our solutions and our products, and were given information on how they were being applied at the same industry at a different time in a different geography.

Hari went on to explain that Ariba leadership managed a global team of 550 sales representatives in three key ways. One was a global sales meeting where everyone came, and it included breakouts about use of their products in different industries. Next was global announcements about big wins in the company, including who led that hunt, so everyone knew how Ariba's influence was growing across borders and industries.

The third piece was internal networking. Apart from the fact that we all got together in similar forums, a lot of camaraderie was built in and encouraged in common teams and common industries. Whether it was virtual meetings, online meetings, in-person meetings or product trainings, you would practically meet every other person in the organization. It was fairly easy for us to have discussions, establish a personal connect, pick up the phone, call people, and share information. In that world, in that environment, it worked well.

—HARI SHANKARANARAYANAN

Ariba paid attention to key concepts in global sales: excellent training, sharing case studies and business outcomes, promoting team knowledge and industry knowledge, and keeping people connected.

Understanding your role as creating the vision and leading the way will keep you on the path to excellence in working with global accounts.

WHALE HUNTING TIPS FOR THE BUYERS' VISION

Vision. The best thing you can offer your customer is a clear vision for what's ahead. Each time you create and hold a vision, you will be more respected by your champion and the buying team and more likely to complete a deal. Initially, this vision may not even be primarily about your product—maybe it removes a stumbling block to a bigger project or builds your reputation as a trusted advisor.

Insight. Work towards gaining insights into your account's problems and opportunities, and then use your insights to bring innovative ideas to the forefront.

Agility. Learn quickly and change direction as your contacts or their company experience changes that make your previous plan outmoded.

Guidance. Be a guide to the buying process. Help your key contacts to understand and convene all of the necessary influencers and lead them on a path to follow in order to reach their decision.

Customer Mindset. More important than anything, cultivate a customer mindset. The more you look at your customers' opportunities and issues rather than your own, the more successful you will be in the arena of global account services.

CHAPTER 12

LOOK AROUND

The test of a first-rate intelligence is the ability to hold two opposed ideas in mind at the same time and still retain the ability to function.

—F. SCOTT FITZGERALD

You will encounter many opposed ideas as you follow your journey through global accounts. One of the most difficult will be focused vs. its opposites, like "aimless" or "scatterbrained." A big chunk of business advice deals with your ability to focus, to set the target, keep the periphery out of view, don't let your mind wander from the job at hand or your company wander from its goals.

Yet everything I've urged you to do seems the opposite of focus, from the curiosity that leads to knowledge to an ecosystem rather than a hierarchy to a process that's beyond steps to a vision instead of a sales message.

So there's the opposition—focus *and* look around. Be a specialist *and* a generalist. On top of that, as Fitzgerald says, don't let it drive you crazy!

One of my favorite business books is Andrew Grove's *Only the Paranoid Survive*. Grove didn't mean his employees should be paranoid or overly fearful, but to have a healthy skepticism about the status quo. That's one of the single most valuable traits that a sales team can provide to their many buyers within a global account: an outside perspective, a contrary point of view.

It's also the best trait that the sales team can bring back home to the executives and product engineers and content marketers. A sense of what's going on out there!

How do you lead a company or a division or department or a team so that your sellers—and by sellers I mean your functional sales team plus all of your subject matter experts who have to be involved in selling and serving a global account—so that your sellers can really offer up a vision, or more important, one vision after another?

Encourage everyone to spend some part of their time looking around! Seriously. Read Popular Science. Tune in to Ovation or the Discovery Channel. Listen to Ted Radio or The New York Public Library podcast. Talk about what's out there with your colleagues and your customers. Look around!

When you learn something new, information is making its way into your brain and integrating with what's already there, and that process changes both what's already there and the new information. Learning is the name we give to that transformation; it is the root of insight and innovation.

Remarkable trends are changing the world of the sellers and the world of the buyers; some that many of us are aware of and others that don't seem relevant to us yet. But these are the things we should all be looking around for, so that we can talk about them intelligently and discuss how changes may influence our customers and industries.

The "Internet of Things" is an example. There's been so much discussion about whether the digital world and social media are making salespeople obsolete. But here's what Tiffani throws into that mix— What happens when things start selling to things?

> *My dishwasher orders my dish washing detergent. I didn't have to go to Costco. I didn't go to Amazon. It might come from one of those places but a thing sold to a thing! It could be big bucks. It could be ... I'm in a manufacturing plant, and my engine is about to die, and the thing sends a message to say you need to send a replacement engine, and that engine is $300,000. It's not just $2.49. It can be big things!*

So how could "things selling to things" influence our future as sellers?

> *Sales leaders are not paying attention to the fact that we could optimize our selling model and sales process by using digital to free up those resources to focus more on these deals you're writing about [in this book] because they're expensive. It's a high cost of sale. It's a longer sale cycle. You need a human being. Why not automate as much as you can and then reallocate those resources to the higher selling, higher average sale price, higher dollar value, more complex sale.*
>
> —TIFFANI BOVA

The word "complex" is problematic because people think digital will only deal with commodity, and the humans will deal with complex sales. Digital can also sell complex things; it depends on the buyer and the circumstance.

Sales strategies will continue to change because everything will continue to change. And the pace of change will continue to increase.

Nevertheless, it is our job to keep creating a vision for our global customers and to report back to our own team what's going on that's different. If you focus exclusively on the issues at hand, you'll lose the outside perspective that your job now requires.

Telematics is another disruption of amazing proportions. The merger of telecommunications and informatics is most associated right now with vehicles, but it's not limited to that.

How does telematics influence your customers? Well, for example, at the end of 2015 Verizon introduced "Hum," a little gadget you can attach to your car that monitors its inner workings and gets you help in an emergency. So here's a massive global company known for phone connectivity moving into the automotive aftermarket. Maybe soon into the original equipment market! Your customers' businesses are morphing.

You know this if you're selling in the auto industry. But can you link it to cellular? What kind of things are getting smarter in your customers' industries, and what could that mean for them? And for your company? Or what does this kind of disruption suggest for your other customers?

How about the Cloud, which enables all this other stuff? It brings huge disruptions to the way we sell certain products and services and creating new challenges for sellers. You used to sell products, like in-house servers, with a very high price tag. Now maybe you sell subscriptions, where the revenue is recurring, so the individual sale is entirely different, your compensation is entirely different, the value proposition is entirely different!

As all of the "things" get smart, we need to get smarter. Not to compete with the smart things, but to use them where we can and use our own intelligence as we sell to and serve our global accounts.

The role of inside sales will continue to grow in global accounts.

The faster things move, the more the buyers will prefer the phone call to the meeting, the text to the email, the digital device to the business lunch.

Hire smart people. Curious people. The ones who want to know why as well as how. Help them learn about your customers, and let them learn from your customers.

When they are working inside a global account, the usual metrics won't matter. The CRM steps don't work. Nothing fits in the same old way.

To be amazingly successful with global accounts, it comes back to the four principles that I started with:

Knowledge—How you learn to know your customers, how you use all your knowledge in service to the customer, and how you build your knowledge base by looking around at what's out there as well as what's inside.

Structure—How you organize your team(s) around the customer's preferences.

Process—How you adapt a step-by-step process to become a realistic account plan for global account sales opportunities

Vision—How you create a vision for your customer, hold it up for them as long as it takes, and lead them on the journey to realize the vision.

With this book, I invite you to differentiate yourself in service to global accounts. To be a company or division or sales team that excels in bridging the disconnect between customers and sellers. To be a distinguished global account whale hunter!

WHALE HUNTING TIPS FOR LOOKING AROUND

Curiosity. Look for trends and innovations outside of your own special field; think of how they might apply to your clients.

Connection. Try actively to connect new information to what's already part of your knowledge base.

Integration. Bring new stuff into your realm of understanding; make it fit with what you already know. You will influence what you know as well as what you learn.

Internal Conversation. Bring new ideas from the outside in to share with your product and service teams. The more you discuss across the silos, the more new ideas you will generate for your customers.

Cross-Functions. Make it a point to spend time listening and learning across functions and across domains within your organization as well as within your customers' organizations.

VISION SUMMARY

This section has explored the role of the lead salesperson in a global account sale. In Whale Hunting lingo, this person is the "harpooner," responsible for keeping the boat close to the whale and leading the hunt. Earlier, when I discussed "hunters" and "farmers," I introduced new definitions for those distinctions among sellers. In Whale Hunting, both the hunters—initial deal sellers—and farmers—global account managers—fulfill the role of harpooner. But the expectations of that role are far from the old, stereotypical definition of a salesperson as a Lone Ranger, a kind of glib rock star—who swoops in and sells the deal by himself through force of will and a gift of gab. Today's successful sellers in global accounts are highly talented leaders of a team of colleagues who follow a fluid process that requires insight and wisdom. They focus on the whale, not on themselves.

What keeps the sales process together and moving forward is a vision, crafted by the sales team on behalf of the client, shared with the client and held out for the client. It's a vision of what's possible, a highly desirable outcome that the customer company—the specific group of buyers – can achieve in concert with the seller company—the specific team of sellers—with whom they are working. The vision is completely customer-centric, but the sales team assumes leadership and does the hard work, whatever it takes, to break through all obstacles that get in the way of achieving the ultimate outcomes that the customer has come to envision.

CONCLUSION

In the final analysis, this book turned out to be primarily about differentiating your company from your competitors through the superior industry knowledge, market knowledge, business knowledge and individual customer knowledge of your salespeople, revealed in their specific interactions with members of the buyers' team. They will be able to apply their knowledge because your sales team has a suitable structure and is closely aligned with a superior field marketing team. They will acquire their knowledge through their own work and collaboration with their team, including their marketing colleagues, through enlightened sales leaders and managers and through impeccably well-planned and well prepared-for interactions with their customers. And they will apply their knowledge through superior leadership of the sales process and a superior vision for their global accounts.

We have seen that companies don't manage global sales well enough. Not only by external measures, but quite simply they don't meet their own expectations. The good ones want to get much, much better, and they are not on a static field. Rather, they are moving at the breakneck speed of modern business along with their clients.

To be a salesperson or a sales leader for global B2B accounts is both a staggering challenge and an enormously rewarding opportunity. I hope this book will inspire you to build some teams, launch some boats, and give new life to some global whales!

Visit my website *http://thewhalehunters.com*
for more resources related to this book.

ABOUT THE EXPERT CONTRIBUTORS

Rachel Barger, GM EMEA & Global Head Customer Success and Value Engineering, Lithium Technologies, Zurich, Switzerland

Rachel Barger has over 15 years' experience in the software industry holding a variety of leadership roles with Professional Services, Customer Success and Enterprise Sales. She brings a global understanding and approach gained through her time spent managing teams in Asia and Europe. Career assignments include Arthur Anderson, Ariba, SAP, and now Lithium Technologies, where she is General Manager for Lithium's European, Middle East and African business unit. Rachel holds a B.S in Chemical Engineering and an MBA from the Australian Graduate School of Management.

Lithium *helps companies unlock the passion of their customers. Lithium software powers amazing Social Customer Experiences for more than 400 iconic brands including AT&T, BT, Best Buy, Indosat, Sephora, Skype and Telstra. Lithium helps companies grow brand advocacy, drive sales, reduce costs and accelerate innovation to create social communities that redefine the customer experience. For more information, visit lithium.com, or connect with them on Twitter, Facebook and their own community – the Lithosphere. Lithium is privately held with corporate headquarters in San Francisco, Calif. and offices in Europe, Asia and Australia.*

Valerie Bonebrake, SVP,Tompkins International
Raleigh, NC and Kansas City, KS USA

Valerie Bonebrake has more than 25 years of industry experience in logistics services. She has worked with an array of companies and industries in North America and across the globe. Valerie was co-founder of YRC Worldwide subsidiary Meridian IQ (now MIQ Logistics), a global third party logistics company, where she served as EVP/COO. Valerie spent 19 years at Ryder Systems, Inc., in various leadership roles of increasing responsibility in the company's supply chain solutions segment. Valerie holds a M.S. in International Logistics from the Georgia Institute of Technology.

__Tompkins International__ is a supply chain consulting and implementation firm that maximizes supply chain performance and value creation. We enable clients to be more profitable and valuable, while also becoming more agile, flexible, and adaptive to the marketplace. Tompkins collaborates with client teams to develop improved operations strategies, supply chain planning, and execution across all the Mega Processes of supply chains (PLAN-BUY-MAKE-MOVE-DISTRIBUTE-SELL), both global and domestic, and from suppliers through to end customers. Tompkins' service lines cover the supply chain strategies, processes, people, and technologies.

Tiffani Bova, VP, Distinguished Analyst and Research Fellow, Gartner
Los Angeles, CA USA

Tiffani Bova is the worldwide lead for Global Go-To-Market / Sales Strategies and Channel Innovation at Gartner. She provides guidance on go to market and sales innovation to the world's largest technology companies and has delivered 200 keynotes to over 250,000 people on 5 continents! Prior to Gartner, Tiffani spent 14 years in various sales, channel and executive roles with start-up and Fortune 500 technology companies. Starting as a quota carrying sales rep, and moving up the ranks she ended her sales career as the head of Gateway Computers indirect channel sales, programs and strategy.

Tiffani was named one of 2014's Most Powerful & Influential Women in California by the National Diversity Council, was voted one of the top 50 Sales and Marketing Influencers by Top Sales World Magazine and INC Magazine Top Sales Leaders to follow on Twitter.

Melissa Donnelly, VP of Sales, JDA
Dallas, TX USA

Melissa Donnelly brings 30 years of experience in selling and managing highly effective sales teams. In her current role, Melissa is responsible for leading JDA's Retail Strategic Accounts team. Prior to JDA, she served as VP of Sales for the Food, Drug and Mass Merchandise sector within NCR. In 2011, she left NCR to join Retalix Ltd. as VP of Sales, where she was responsible for leading the retail software and services sales team for North America, a role she held until the acquisition of Retalix by NCR in 2013.

Melissa is based out of Dallas where she lives with her husband and two children.

Gerhard Gschwandtner, Founder and CEO, *Selling Power* Magazine and Sales 2.0 Conferences, Fredericksburg, VA USA

 *Gerhard Gschwandtner established his professional reputation as a sales guru by training over 10,000 salespeople in Europe and the US. Realizing that sales-people and their managers need all the help they can get, he started* **Selling Power** *magazine and turned it into the world's leading sales management mag-azine. Gerhard's mission is to contribute to the success of sales leaders with SellingPower.com, a sales intelligence platform that's visited by over 300,000 sales leaders every month.*

Gerhard runs four Sales 2.0 conferences a year (in Philadelphia, Boston, San Francisco and Las Vegas) that attract over 1,200 sales and marketing leaders. These conferences are based on sharing ideas through unscripted conversations and continuous exploration of the core theme: improving people, enhancing processes and implementing advanced technology solutions to achieve operational efficiency and greater customer satisfaction. (www.sales20conf.com)

Jeff Hargroves, President, ProPharma Group, LLC
Kansas City, Kansas USA

Jeff Hargroves founded ProPharma Group in 2001. His vision was to create a company that would serve clients long term, creating a partnership to provide compliance-related solutions in an innovative manner. Jeff has held positions in Operations, Quality Assurance and Engineering for manufacturing and consulting companies in the drug industry. He is actively involved in the Parenteral Drug Association, International Society of Pharmaceutical Engineers and Regulatory Affairs Professional Society and earned the BS in Computer Engineering and the BS in Electrical Engineering from the University of Missouri.

When clients need to navigate the complicated and changing regulatory environment, ProPharma Group is their first choice. They put their unique combination of leading industry knowledge, breadth of experience, and proven processes to work —providing the information their customers need to deliver safe, effective and quality products every time. At ProPharma Group, their reputation is built on protecting yours.

Matt Heinz, President, Heinz Marketing
Seattle, WA USA

Matt Heinz has more than 15 years of marketing, business development and sales experience from a variety of organizations, vertical industries and company sizes. He has held various positions at companies including Microsoft, Weber Shandwick, Boeing, The Seattle Mariners, Market Leader and Verdiem. In 2007, Matt began Heinz Marketing to help clients focus their business on market and customer opportunities, then execute a plan to scale revenue and customer growth.

Matt's specialties include marketing, sales, demand generation, social media, public relations, brand management, business development, strategic management, customer experience, and strategy.

Jill Konrath, Keynote Speaker, Award-Winning Author, Sales Accelerator, Minneapolis, MN USA

Jill Konrath is passionate about helping salespeople and entrepreneurs be more successful in today's ever-changing business environment. She delivers interactive presentations and workshops that help people accelerate their sales and win more deals.

Jill's expertise has been featured in Fortune, Forbes, The New York Times, ABC News, Wall Street Journal, Entrepreneur, Fox2, Inc and many other media outlets. Her newsletters are read by 125,000+ sellers worldwide and her popular blog has been syndicated on numerous business and sales websites.

Jill speaks at sales kick-offs, annual sales meetings, conferences and industry associations, including Dreamforce (SalesForce.com), SalesConnect (LinkedIn.) and InBound (HubSpot).

Jill is the author of 3 bestselling sales books:

- ***Agile Selling*** *focuses on the mindset & skills needed to stay at the top of your game.*

- ***SNAP Selling*** *highlights strategies that work with today's savvy, busy buyers*

- ***Selling to Big Companies*** *helps salespeople create new and larger opportunities*

Sid Kumar, Global Head of Inside Sales, CA Technologies
New York, NY USA

Sid Kumar is the global head of inside sales at CA Technologies, where he leads a team of sales and presales professionals to accelerate growth for the company. He is an accomplished leader and operating executive in the technology sector with extensive general management and P&L experience.

Previously, he formed and led the Customer Lifecycle Solutions organization to help enterprises maximize the value of their software investments through proactive portfolio management. Prior to this role, Sid led global operations for the $2.5 billion Mainframe Solutions business and served as the divisional CFO for the $100 million Internet Security Business Unit. He has also held corporate leadership roles across strategy, operations, finance and business development.

Prior to joining CA Technologies, Sid led venture capital & private equity investments and drove M&A and capital markets transactions across the technology sector. Sid holds a M.B.A. in strategic management from The Wharton School and a B.A. in economics from Yale University. He lives in Long Island, New York with his wife, Sejal, and his two children, Pavan & Nikita.

Lisa Magnuson, Founder and Corporate Sales Strategist, Top Line Sales, Portland, OR USA

Lisa Magnuson is an expert in corporate strategic sales and TOP Line Account™ revenue building. Lisa works with clients to build successful strategic sales programs that drive revenue from large new accounts and enable growth from existing high value customers. She has worked with clients large and small across a broad spectrum of industries including high technology, healthcare, software, manufacturing and professional services. She also draws on her background of holding executive positions with Xerox Corporation and IKON Office Solutions as well as serving on high profile Boards including the Portland State University Foundation Board of Directors.

Books by Lisa Magnuson include:

- *The Simple Executive Engagement Plan*
- *3 Secrets to Increase Sales with Existing Customers*
- *The 48-Hour Rule™*

The TOP Line Account Way™ is a strategic framework for developing and closing TOP Line Account™ opportunities. It includes methodologies and tools scalable to any sized customer or prospect. The system overlays a company's normal sales process and integrates throughout the sales cycle. http://toplinesales.com

214

Kirk Robinson, SVP Commercial Markets Division &
Global Accounts, Ingram Micro, Orange County, CA USA

Kirk Robinson has been SVP of Commercial Markets and Global Accounts for North America at Ingram Micro since 2013. Prior to that he has served in many leadership positions at Ingram Micro including VP and GM Commercial Markets Division, VP of Value-added Reseller and GovEd sales market development and business intelligence, VP of Channel Marketing, and more. He has 13-years experience in Ingram Micro sales and marketing.

Ingram Micro helps businesses realize the promise of technology. It delivers the full spectrum of global technology and supply chain services to businesses around the world. Ingram Micro's global infra-structure and deep expertise in technology solutions, cloud, supply chain solutions and mobility enable its business partners to operate efficiently and successfully in the markets they serve. Unrivaled agility, deep market insights and the trust and dependability that comes from decades of proven relationships, set Ingram Micro apart and ahead.

Mircea Saracut, Head of Business Development—EMEAA, Symbicore
Cluj County, Romania

Mircea Saracut has been selling to the world's top companies for twenty years, including E.ON, Emerson, Vodafone, AIG and others. Mircea has also been strategically and tactically guiding people to become sales professionals who can also sell to the world's top companies. He has achieved two MBA's, in Business Administration and Economics, and has been trained as an engineer. Over the course of twenty years, Mircea has become one of Europe's best educated, government accredited sales professionals.

Symbicore is a global branding, marketing, and digital design partner to trusted businesses around the world. Symbicore's team of experts has proven track record in providing a full suite of integrated business tools helping the development of businesses across a wide range of industries.

Symbicore delivers Marketing Intelligence, Inbound and Outbound Marketing, Social Media Optimization, Customer Care Outsourcing and Management.

216

Hari Shankaranarayanan, Managing Director with a leading management consulting services company, New Dehli, India

Hari Shankaranarayanan has 17+ years of experience across consulting, and outsourcing with expertise in organization strategy, process transformation and cost reduction. In his current role, Hari works with leading Resources organizations in shaping their transformation agenda.

In the past Hari has worked with Ariba leading their sales & consulting services in India & Australia and also worked with the Essar Group as part of the founding & leadership team of Essar's Shared Services.

Hari's specialties include P&L management, sales, business development, global delivery, and consulting. He works in the Supply Chain Management, Procurement, and Operations domains.

Dr. Greg Story, President, Dale Carnegie Training Japan
Tokyo, Japan

Originally from Australia, Greg came to Japan for a two-year post-graduate study but remained for 30 years, working in international real estate, Australia-Japan trade, and retail banking targeting high net worth customers. His interests in start-ups, turnarounds and corporate strategy led him to Dale Carnegie Training Japan, where he helps companies dealing with these issues. Greg holds a Masters Degree from Jochi (Sophia) University and a Ph.D. from Griffith University in International Relations/Political Science. He is a Board member of the International Dale Carnegie Franchisee Association and has given almost 500 keynote speeches, most of which were in Japanese.

Greg is Podcast host of "THE Leadership Japan Series" on iTunes, and among many honors and recognitions he is Emeritus Chairman of both the Australia-New Zealand Chamber of Commerce In Japan and the Queensland-Japan Chamber of Commerce

The Dale Carnegie Training Japan team offers tailored solutions for companies, utilizing 104 years of constant refinement and responsiveness to customer requirements, partnered with sharing of cutting edge experience across over 97 countries, which keeps Dale Carnegie Training at the forefront of the training business.

ABOUT THE AUTHOR

Dr. Barbara Weaver Smith is founder and CEO of The Whale Hunters® and co-author of *Whale Hunting: How to Land Big Sales and Transform Your Company*, based on the collaborative culture of the Inuit people who engaged their entire village to hunt whales. Barbara teaches companies to rapidly increase their revenue through **bigger sales to bigger customers**. She supports her clients' success with a steady stream of new content for consulting, speaking, and online training.

Barbara is in her third career. First she was an English professor, where she learned the art of sales from the rhetoric of its founder, Aristotle. She became a college dean before leaving academia for her second career as president as a statewide nonprofit agency affiliated with the National Endowment for the Humanities. Her eclectic background has given her more than 20 years' of rich experience in leading diverse groups of stakeholders to create purposeful, high stakes deals for education and community projects. In 1994, she took the entrepreneurial plunge and brought her knowledge and skills into the for-profit world.

Barbara's project diversity and her first-hand leadership background in each economic sector make her especially skilled at bridging the gaps among corporate silos and cultures to build powerful cross-functional teams that achieve superior revenue goals.

Barbara works with small and midsize companies to build the seamless processes that guarantee their continued growth, revenue, and profits and position them to compete with larger competitors for global customers. She also works with large corporations who struggle to organize the kind of internal cooperative culture that they need in order to become trusted advisors to and continually grow their business with their key accounts, including global accounts.

Barbara is a graduate of Anderson University and earned the M.A. and Ph.D. at Ball State University. She was named Sagamore of the Wabash, Indiana's highest civilian honor, for exceptional community programs throughout the state. She lives in the Phoenix, Arizona, metropolitan area.

Visit *http://thewhalehunters.com*

To have Barbara speak to your sales team

To sign up for a Global Sales event

To explore training opportunities, live and online

ALSO BY BARBARA WEAVER SMITH

Whale Hunting: How to Land Big Sales and Transform Your Company

"Whale Hunting is a remarkable book that outlines a process for anyone in sales to land big clients. Be prepared to turn traditional sales processes upside down. Whale hunting is not about sheer strength, but about vision, focus, determination, agility, and a role for everyone. Barbara Weaver Smith tells us how to hunt the whale as if our life depended on it – and it does."

—JOANNE S. BLACK
NOMORECOLDCALLING.COM

Mind of a Hunter reinforces the need for focus during a whale hunt. Each villager must know what each Inuit whale hunter knew: the whale is worth the trouble. No amount of distraction, fear, boredom, or nostalgia can be allowed to clutter the minds of the whale hunters eager to capture an account that will move your company to the next level.

The Hunt introduces you to some of the unexpected ways a whale company can slip from the grasp of those small companies that are not able to hold the right tension on the harpoon line. Don't let the whale slip away from you. Learn the ways of the whale, the wind, and the water.

Riding the Whale explains why companies behave the way they do in the middle of your sales process and what you can do about it. In this volume, The Whale Hunters share their experiences and reflect on what it is like to ride the whale to successful completion of the hunt.

Whale Hunting Culture demonstrates that the entire village must be ready to harvest the whale as soon as you beach it—meaning the contract is signed. This volume offers methods to ensure that you can encourage a fast-growth culture that can properly deliver your services to a whale account.

All books available at amazon.com and other vendors.

Made in United States
Orlando, FL
22 January 2022